Make Room
for the Boom . . .
or Bust

Gary L. McIntosh is associate professor of practical theology and the director of the Doctor of Ministry program at Talbot School of Theology. An experienced church consultant, he has analyzed more than 500 churches in 53 denominations and has conducted more than 130 workshops dealing with the topic of church growth. He is currently president of the American Society for Church Growth and editor of the *Church Growth Network* newsletter and *The Journal of American Church Growth*.

In 1989 Dr. McIntosh founded the Church Growth Network, a consulting firm that assists churches to reach their greatest effectiveness in finding, keeping, and building people. The Church Growth Network conducts individual church consultations with specialization in the areas of generational change, analysis of church health, and five-year planning.

For complete information, contact Dr. Gary L. McIntosh at

> The Church Growth Network
> 3630 Camellia Drive
> San Bernardino, CA 92404
> (909) 882-5386
> gary_mcintosh@peter.biola.edu

By Gary L. McIntosh
Three Generations
The Exodus Principle
How to Develop a Policy Manual
How to Develop a Pastoral Compensation Plan

**By Gary L. McIntosh
and Rodney Dean**
How to Start Small Groups

**By Gary L. McIntosh
and Glen S. Martin**
The Issachar Factor
Finding Them, Keeping Them

Make Room
for the Boom . . .
or Bust

*Six Church Models
for Reaching Three Generations*

Gary L. McIntosh

Fleming H. Revell
A Division of Baker Book House
Grand Rapids, Michigan 49516

Published by Fleming H. Revell
a division of Baker Book House Company
P.O. Box 6287, Grand Rapids, MI 49516-6287

Printed in the United States of America

Library of Congress Cataloging-in-Publication Data

McIntosh, Gary, 1947–
    Make room for the boom . . . or bust : six church models for reaching three generations / Gary L. McIntosh.
      p. cm.
    Includes bibliographical references.
    ISBN 0-8007-5614-2
    1. Evangelistic work—United States. 2. Pastoral theology—United States. 3. Baby boom generation—Religious life. 4. Generation X—Religious life. 5. United States—Religion—1960– I. Title.
    BV3793.M35 1997
    253′.0973—dc20   96-35828

To C. Ed Schneider
1940–1996
Mentor, colleague, and friend

Contents

Acknowledgments

The initial stimulus for this book came from Rev. Harry D. Williams, former Church Growth director of the California Southern Baptist Convention. In 1990 Harry invited me to speak at five pastors' conferences on the distinctives of Builders, Boomers, and Busters. I eagerly accepted his invitation.

The Southern Baptists enjoyed phenomenal success in reaching the pre–World War II displaced Southerners and Mid-Westerners who moved to California in the 1950s and 1960s. However, a study in 1988 revealed that 74 percent of the Southern Baptist churches in California were either plateaued or declining in membership. At that time the average California Southern Baptist was about 58 years old, while the median age in the state was only 35.7.

Building on a desire to effectively "make disciples" (Matt. 28:19), the conference on "Innovative Approaches to Reaching the Unchurched California Culture" was designed. It was while speaking at this conference that I first learned about five types of churches that the Church Growth Division had identified as demonstrating success in reaching the younger generations.

I asked Harry if anyone was going to publish their research in a popular version for churches outside the Southern Baptist Convention, and he suggested that I might be the best one to do it. Since that time, I've completed further research and expanded on the models first presented at those conferences. However, I am indebted to Harry and his research staff for their original discovery of these church models.

My appreciation also goes to my editor, William J. Petersen, who, after reading some of my articles on generational change, asked me to write a book on Builders, Boomers, and Busters for Revell. It was in that initial book, *Three Generations,* that I first mentioned the models now fully developed in *Make Room for the Boom . . . or Bust.* I'm thankful for Bill's gracious encouragement and support through-out both of these projects.

In addition, my gratitude goes to my copyeditor on both *Three Generations* and *Make Room for the Boom . . . or Bust,* Mary L. Suggs. Her expertise has added immeasurably to the quality and readability of my writing, for which I'm certain you the reader will be thankful.

My gratitude is also extended to my administrative assistant, Carolyn Crawford, who ably watched over the Talbot Doctor of Ministry program while I was on sabbatical, completing this book.

I'm further grateful to Pastors Tim Celek, David Page, Tim Ellis, Glen Martin, Sam Williams, and Jim Meyer who each have contributed a chapter to this book. Their willingness to take time from busy schedules to write candidly about their church experience adds a measure of reality to the models of ministry presented.

Finally, my loving gratitude goes to my wife for enduring too many piles of paper around the house while I wrote this manuscript. Now that I'm finished, I'll pick up all the papers and keep my desk clean, at least until the next manuscript. Carol, thanks for partnering with me in this ministry. You're the love of my life.

Over the Hill to Grandma's House

Three years ago I was lecturing on Builders, Boomers, and Busters at a pastors' conference in Southern California. The speaker who followed me began his comments by saying, "I'm not a Boomer or Buster. I don't want to be a Boomer or Buster. In fact, I don't even like Boomers and Busters!"

While he used that opening to get the audience's attention, I've since discovered that the speaker is like many of you who may be reading this book. All the emphasis on Boomers and Busters—what they wear, where they live, who they vote for, when they take vacations, what style of music they listen to—has made you a little ill.

I can relate to that feeling. It seems that when a trend is over-publicized, it can become almost nauseating. Why can't we simply minister to everyone in a general way like we always have in the past? Honestly, are we not all just sinners who need Christ? Why spend the time and energy focusing on the differences of each generation?

Yes, the Builder, Boomer, and Buster generations are alike in their need for Christ. Yet we must admit that in many ways the generations are quite different. It is these differences that make it necessary to establish new models of ministry in order to effectively evangelize each generation. Developing new forms of church ministry is nothing new. It has happened before and is taking place once again. The church is, and in a sense always has been, just one generation away from extinction. Throughout the centuries, as each new generation has emerged, the church has communicated the timeless gospel in a new way. It has reinvented itself to speak to a new audience that perceives and thinks differently than the generations before it.

Generation Gaps

The need for new models of ministry became evident to me a few years ago when I was visiting my ninety-four-year-old grandmother in Colorado Springs, Colorado. At that time she lived alone in her own house right next door to my mother. While visiting my grandmother, I walked into her bathroom and noticed on the counter a clear plastic bottle full of little pieces of soap. It appeared to be an empty dish detergent bottle. My grandmother had used all of the dish detergent, washed out the bottle, and removed the label from the front. Over several months, she had deposited small pieces of bath soap in it. She then filled the bottle with water and let it sit, letting the soap dissolve. When she took her bath or washed her hands, rather than use a new bar of soap, she extended the use of those end pieces of soap by using the soapy water.

Curious to know why she took the trouble to save little pieces of soap, I went to the living room where my grandmother was sitting and asked, "Grandma, what is that bottle of soap pieces doing in your bathroom?" "Well, Gary," she replied, "you know in the Depression we had a saying, 'Use it up, thin it out, make it last, or do without,' and I want to use up every little bit of soap."

Somewhat surprised, I blurted out, "But Grandma, it's not the Depression; it's the 1990s and you have plenty of money! You can just buy a new bar of soap whenever you need one." Without hesitation she countered, "That's true now, Gary, but you just never know when things will change."

Three days later, next door at my mother's house, I opened the door of a large closet next to the bathroom where she keeps all her towels, washcloths, soaps, and cleaners. Reaching for a towel, I noticed two cases of bathroom spray cleaner sitting on the floor. A total of twenty-four spray cans of bathroom cleaner! Thinking it odd to have such a large stockpile of bathroom cleaner on hand, I went to my mother and asked, "Mom! What's with all the bathroom cleaner in your closet?" She answered, "I was shopping at K-Mart a week or two ago, and they had the best price on bathroom spray cleaner that I had ever seen. I thought to myself, *you never know when you are going to need a can of bathroom cleaner.* So I bought two cases."

My grandmother and mother belong to the Builder generation. Both lived in Oklahoma during the Great Depression years. My mother married during World War II just before my father left for the war. One of her major memories of that time was the rationing that took place. Throughout their lives, both carried strong memories of poor economic conditions. They recalled times of struggle when one made things last, stored items for future use, or simply went without.

As a member of the Boomer generation, I grew up in a different environment. Instead of experiencing lean economic years, I enjoyed a time of economic boom in the United States in the 1950s and 1960s. When I use bath soap to the point that it's just a little end piece, I throw it in the trash. I can always buy another bar of soap, so why try to use the little end pieces? In my house we have two bathrooms. We have two cans of bathroom cleaner, one under the sink in each bathroom. Since we can easily purchase more at our local grocery store, we never think of storing up cleaner in case of an emergency.

My children, who are part of the Buster generation, view life in a slightly different way. They, of course, throw away the little end pieces of soap just as I do. Actually they hardly give a thought to the end pieces of soap. Their concern is whether or not the soap is biodegradable. They do not want to harm the environment. Their concern is not whether we have enough cans of spray cleaner. Their concern is whether the spray can has chlorofluorocarbons in it that will hurt the ozone layer.

My family has the same religious background, generally the same theology, and similar core values. We all love the Lord and care about his church. Yet the three generations have a slightly different perception of life that leads us to enjoy different types of churches. Throughout the generations my family has been found worshiping in a small country church in Oklahoma to a mega church in Southern California. My grandmother and mother would never have felt at home in a mega church. Likewise, my children most likely would find it strange to be in a small country church. We have all responded to Christ in churches that faithfully presented the gospel message but through contrasting forms and styles.

Generational Contrasts

The generational contrasts in my family represent just the surface of a more complicated issue.[1] There are many differences between the generations. Some of them are given in the following chart.

Builders	Boomers	Busters
High birth rate	Low birth rate	Higher birth rate (than Boomers)
High view of marriage	Low view of marriage	Higher view of marriage
Low divorce rate	High divorce rate	Lower divorce rate
Early marriage	Late marriage	Later marriage
Family strong	Family weak	Family stronger
Traditional roles	Changing roles	Return to traditional roles
Respect authority	Question authority	Ignore authority
Private	Open	Cautious
Save items	Throw items away	Recycle items
Complete tasks	Partly complete tasks	Tasks left undone

I include in the Builder generation those people born before 1946. They survived three wars, a national economic depression, and tough economic times. Through it all they built families, homes, churches, and the greatest nation in the world. Due to the slow pace of change and the common social issues they faced during their formative years, this generation tends to perceive life in the same basic way.

The Boomer generation is made up of children of the Builders. Born between 1946 and 1964, this generation developed quite a different perspective on life. They challenged their families, colleges, and government throughout the 60s and 70s. Today the Boomer generation is middle-aged. The oldest turned fifty-one years old in 1997 and close to four million Boomers will turn fifty years old every year until 2014! The largest generation that the United States has ever known, they will greatly affect our world on into the year 2030.

The third generation is the children of the Boomers and the grand-children of the Builders. They are referred to as Busters since they are a smaller generational group than that of their Boomer parents. The Busters are quite literally the most neglected, lonely, hurting generation we have ever seen in the United States. A generation of latchkey kids, Busters were often neglected by their Boomer parents. Many are not ready to serve the Lord Jesus Christ because they must deal with emotional baggage before they will have the energy to minister in our churches.

Each of these generations has distinct viewpoints regarding church life that make it difficult to reach them all with the same church model. Note the different viewpoints on some selected aspects of church life below.

Builders	Boomers	Busters
Committed to church	Committed to relationships	Committed to family
Program-oriented	People-oriented	Community-oriented
Money to missions	Money to people	Money to causes
In-depth Bible study and prayer	Practical Bible study, prayer/share	Issue-oriented Bible study, prayer/share
Loyalty to denomination	Loyalty to people	Loyalty to family
Minister out of duty	Minister for satisfaction	Minister to meet needs
Desire stability	Desire creativity	Desire variety
Expect formality	Expect informality	Expect spontaneity
Enjoy Sunday school	Enjoy small groups	Enjoy family atmosphere
Hymns	Praise songs	Variety of music
Expository sermons	"How to" sermons	Practical sermons
Pastoral prayer	Various people pray	Family group prays
Guests recognized	Guests anonymous	Guests respected
Organ/piano	Guitars/drums	Jazz ensemble
Low participation	Higher participation	Some participation

Except for churches that have been planted in the last few years, most existing churches in the United States were established to evangelize, assimilate, and disciple the Builder generation. The perspective on church life pictured in the above column under Builders would comfortably describe most existing churches today.

However, as we can see by looking at the columns under Boomers and Busters, these two generations have new expectations for church life (see table at end of this chapter for a complete overview). These newer expectations have led to the development of new models of church ministry in an effort to reach and keep the younger generations. We are concerned, of course, for all three generational groups. However, since most churches are already designed to reach the Builder generation, a strong need exists to establish new models of church ministry to reach the Boomer and Buster generations.

Six New Models

Like most people, in my early years as a Christian I had a very limited view of churches. I became a Christian as a junior high school student and quickly became involved in the life of my church. Since my church experience was very narrow, to me there was only one way to do church—the way I had experienced it! Little did I know that there were other valid ways of church ministry. Later through a variety of circumstances, I discovered that God creatively uses many different styles, forms, and models of church ministry.

Over the last fourteen years I've had the opportunity to travel across the United States leading seminars and workshops on several topics related to church growth. In addition, I've analyzed more than five hundred churches, offering each one suggestions on how to be more effective in fulfilling the mandate to "make disciples" (Matt. 28:19). These experiences provided opportunities to see different models of church ministry and to discuss each one with pastors and church members. I've found that there are at least six new models of church ministry that are effectively reaching Boomers and Busters. However, many church leaders are aware of only two— the seeker-centered and the seeker-sensitive models. The seeker-centered model has been popularized by Willow Creek Community Church in South Barrington, Illinois. The seeker-sensitive model has been described by George Barna in his book *User Friendly Churches.*[2] These two models have similar characteristics but are different in several ways. I will discuss these models in chapters five through eight. There are four additional models—blended model, multiple-track model, satellite model, and rebirthed model—that are not as well known. I will describe each one in chapters nine through sixteen. Along with the descriptions, a study of each model will be shared so that you can see how the model is played out in a real-life situation. Each of the case studies is told in the words of a pastor from a church of that model. Due to my familiarity with churches in California, I selected representative churches from this area of the country. However, examples of all the models discussed can be found throughout the country.

One approach that has been widely used to develop new church models that relate to the new generations is the church-planting model. I've chosen not to discuss this model here since it has been covered adequately in many other books, manuals, and seminars. If you're interested in planting a new church, I highly recommend the materials written by my good friend, Dr. Robert E. Logan.[3]

The purpose of writing *Make Room for the Boom . . . or Bust* is to introduce all six models so that church leaders may wisely choose the best model for their church. But before we begin to discuss each model, it is necessary to indulge in a bit of groundwork. Chapters two through four will focus on the openness of the Boomer and Buster generations to the gospel and the development of key principles for reaching them for Christ. After we overview each new model, we'll conclude with insights on how to transform an existing church into a starkly different one to reach the aging Boomer and emerging Buster generations.

To get the most out of this book, you should read all of the chapters. If you find you have a special interest in a particular model, read that chapter first and the accompanying case study and begin to use some of the ideas and insights suggested. Then go back and read the other chapters to expand your understanding of the other models available to you and your church. Whatever model you choose to use, I pray that God will direct your decisions, plans, and application of this material to effectively "make disciples" of Builders, Boomers, Busters, and all future generations (Ps. 90:1).

Comparison of Generations 1997

Factors	Builders	Boomers	Busters
Ages	52 + years	33 to 51 years old	14 to 32 years old
Names	Strivers and Survivors	Challengers	Calculators
	Suppies (senior, urban professionals)	Yuppies (young, urban professionals)	Yiffies (young, individual- istic, freedom-minded, and few)
	Opals (older people with active lifestyles)	Grumpies (grim, ruthless professionals)	13ers (13th generation from founding fathers)
	Rappies (retired, affluent professionals)	Yuffies (young, urban failures)	Posties (Post-Boomer generation)
	Woofs (well-off older folks)	Oinks (one income, no kids) Dinks (double income, no kids) Dinkwads (double income, no kids with a dog)	
	Whoopies (well- heeled older people)	New Collars (information workers) Gold Collars (high paid infor- mation workers)	
	Grumpies (grown-up mature people)	Would Be's (would like to be yuppies)	
	War Babies (born 1940–45)	Postwar Babies	Echo Boom Baby Boomlet
	Seniors	Hermes (hermits from friends, life in general)	
	G.I. Generation Silent Generation	Vietnam Generation Postwar Generation Sixties Generation Me Generation	Generation X The Reagan Generation
		Thirtysomethings Fortysomethings	Twentysomethings
Formative Years	1920s, 30s, 40s	1950s, 60s, 70s	1980s, 90s, 2000s

Comparison of Generations 1997 *(continued)*

Factors	Builders	Boomers	Busters
Formative Events	Rural lifestyle	Suburbia	Back to city/country
	Radio	T.V.	Cable T.V./video
	Automobile	Airplane	Internet
	WW I/WW II/ Korea	Vietnam	Persian Gulf War
	Low technology	Growing technology	High technology
	The Great Depression	Economic affluence	Variable economy
	Pearl Harbor	Assassinations	*Challenger* disaster
	Big bands and jazz	Rock-n-Roll	Variety of music
	Family, school, church	College	Peer group, work
	The Roaring Twenties	Cold war	Berlin Wall dismantled
	The New Deal	Civil rights movement	Impact of *Roe v. Wade*
	Rationing	The New Frontier and space race	AIDS
	The atomic bomb	Energy crisis	The O.J. trial
	FDR Administration	Watergate and Nixon resignation	The Clinton administration
Characteristics	High birth rate	Low birth rate	Higher birth rate (than Boomers)
	High view of marriage	Low view of marriage	Higher view of marriage
	Low divorce rate	High divorce rate	Lower divorce rate
	Early marriage	Late marriage	Later marriage
	Family strong	Family weak	Family stronger
	Limited education	High education	Practical education
	Respect authority	Question authority	Ignore authority
	Private	Open	Cautious
	Save everything	Throw away everything	Recycle everything
	Complete tasks	Partly complete tasks	Tasks left undone
	Audio orientation	Tuned in to all media	Visual orientation

Comparison of Generations 1997 *(continued)*

Factors	Builders	Boomers	Busters
Religious Factors	Commitment to Christ = commitment to church	Commitment to Christ = commitment to relationships	Commitment to Christ = commitment to family
	Program-oriented	People-oriented	Community-oriented
	Money to missions	Money to people	Money to causes
	In-depth Bible study and prayer	Practical Bible study, prayer/share	Issue-oriented Bible study, prayer/share
	Loyalty to denomination	Loyalty to people	Loyalty to family
	Minister out of duty	Minister for personal satisfaction	Minister to meet needs
	Support missions	Support big causes	Support local causes
Programs	Relate to missions	Relate to people	Relate to family
	Stress in-depth Bible study and prayer	Stress fellowship and support groups	Stress Bible studies on issues
	Maintain stability	Be creative	Use variety
	Focus on marriage and grandparenting	Focus on marriage and family	Focus on marriage and singles
	Be formal	Be relational	Be spontaneous
	Encourage involvement with Busters	Encourage involvement in small groups	Encourage involvment in community issues
Worship	Quiet	Talkative	Noisy
	Hymns	Praise songs	Variety of music
	Expository sermons	"How to" sermons	Practical sermons
	Pastoral prayer	Various people pray	Leaders pray
	Guests recognized	Guests anonymous	Guests respected
	Organ/piano	Guitars/drums	Jazz ensembles/ small bands
	Reverence	Celebration	Fun
	Long attention spans	Short attention spans	Shorter attention spans
	Formality	Casual	Laid back
	Predictable pace	Fast pace	Quicker pace
	Soft music	Loud music	Louder music

Comparison of Generations 1997 (continued)

Factors	Builders	Boomers	Busters
Implica-tions for Future	Ability to carry on programs and projects will wane	Support of people-oriented projects will continue	More involve-ment with issue-oriented projects
	Giving will continue until retirement	Giving will be related to people projects	Giving will be related to issues and causes
	Revivalistic evan-gelism will con-tinue to decline	Friendship evan-gelism will con-tinue strong	12-step evan-gelism events will grow
	Loyalty to institu-tions will continue to decline	Loyalty to people will continue strong	Loyalty to family and local causes will grow

2

Take My BMW, Please

Who is Kathleen Casey Wilkins? Need a clue? She was born in Philadelphia at one second past midnight on January 1, 1946. Still stumped? She is America's first Boomer. She's also the first member of America's largest generation to turn fifty-one years old in 1997! On January 1, 1997, about seven thousand Boomers turned fifty-one. The generation that once proclaimed it is better to burn out than rust out, to die before you get old, and to not trust anyone over thirty, today is between the ages of thirty-three and fifty-one.[1] And they hate it.

In 1996 a Boomer turned fifty every 8.4 seconds. By 2001, one will turn fifty every 6.8 seconds in the United States. From now until the year 2010, nearly four million Boomers will reach the milestone annually (see figure 1). The generation that cut its teeth on *Howdy Doody* and the *Mickey Mouse Club* will soon find that the candles and cakes will bring new aches, pains, diseases, and doubts. As each one turns fifty he or she will soon receive a greeting in the mail announcing guaranteed acceptance for membership in the AARP, the American Association of Retired Persons. "Retired persons" are also often known as "senior citizens."

Middle Adulthood

Life for a particular Boomer couple I know was especially tough for a couple of years. Her father died in April 1994. His mother died in January 1995. In July their close friend killed himself after he apparently let his high-pressure job get the best of him. They both started new jobs and their daughter is going through adolescence. He's fifty; she's forty-nine—successful, midlife Boomers on the lead-

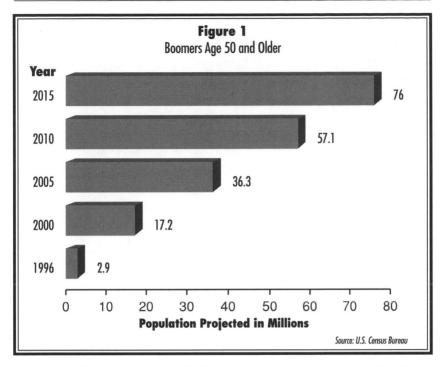

Figure 1
Boomers Age 50 and Older

Year
2015 — 76
2010 — 57.1
2005 — 36.3
2000 — 17.2
1996 — 2.9

0 10 20 30 40 50 60 70 80
Population Projected in Millions

Source: U.S. Census Bureau

ing edge of a demographic bulge. It's only a coincidence that he is president of the United States and she was in charge of renovating the nation's health care system. Any member of their generation may have experienced things similar to what Bill and Hillary Clinton experienced since they changed jobs.

For past generations this time was called middle age. For Boomers it's being renamed "middle adulthood." Adulthood roughly covers the period from twenty to eighty years old. The midpoint of those years is fifty. Even though Boomers turning fifty will qualify for membership in AARP, their self-image is anything but a "senior." "Am I going to sign up? It isn't on my list of priorities," says film critic Gene Siskel, who turned fifty on January 26, 1996. "I just had a baby boy, I just shot from half court at the Bulls game and hit the rim twice. . . ."[2]

"We're going to change the way midlife is seen," says William Pollack, a men's health specialist at Harvard Medical School. "Historically, we've seen fifty as over the hill. As baby boomers, we're going to try not to allow that."[3]

Since Boomers who turn fifty are likely to live another twenty-seven years—women almost thirty-two—there's every reason for them to remain active and to continue doing what they've been doing so far. The truth is that we're dealing with old numbers. Fifty doesn't mean what it used to mean. Eighty doesn't mean what it used to. To determine the attitudes of aging Boomers, the Del Webb Corporation surveyed one thousand people born in 1946 and found that the median age the respondents considered old was seventy-nine.[4]

Exactly when does middle age creep up? A new joke that surfaced about 1992 described the four ages of man: You believe in Santa Claus; you don't believe in Santa Claus; you are Santa Claus; and you look like Santa Claus. A more serious analysis by Dr. Win Arn, an expert on the aging of America, gives five stages of adulthood.

Emerging Adults	18–30 years
Young Adults	30–50 years
Middle Adults	50–70 years
Senior Adults	70–80 years
Elderly Adults	80+ years[5]

What does it mean to be middle-aged? According to a survey by the American Board of Family Practice, you are middle-aged if you

- are between forty-six and sixty-five years old
- think more about the past than the future
- don't recognize the names of new music groups
- need a day or two to recover from strenuous exercise
- worry about having money to take care of future medical needs[6]

Dr. Jim Conway, author of the popular book *Men in Mid-Life Crisis,* suggests that "mid-life today is defined not by what it is but by what it is between. The man in mid-life is caught between adolescent children and his aging parents."[7] The squeeze on middle-aged Boomers is felt from below as Busters press for power and advancement, and from above as Builders cry for assistance and care.

Signs of Aging

Boomers obviously are entering the middle adult years. For some it means a second young adulthood, but for others it means coming face-to-face with the typical challenges of that life stage. If middle age means the mid-years of one's adult life, and if life expectancy is the mid-seventies, the middle years, technically, range from about thirty-seven to fifty-five. And it certainly is true that these years bring some undesirable physical changes. The signs of middle age are familiar: diminished eyesight, brittle bones, slowed reflexes, and tendons that lack resilience.

Physical Signs

The Big M. Boomers have gone through a lot of change. For Boomer women it's now The Change. The first of forty million Boomer women are crossing the hormonal divide—menopause— the Big M. Men are not far behind. "Nipping and Tucking," a recent article in the December 1995 issue of *Forbes,* reports that Boomer men are going to plastic surgeons for hair transplants, erasing facial wrinkles and sagging eyelids, eliminating "turkey gobbler" chins, and even undergoing liposuction of pot bellies and love handles.[8]

Gravity is reality. Blue jeans, for generations the uniform of rebels and conformists alike, began fading from the fashion forefront as Boomers began to look for new and more flattering looks. Jeans didn't fit the lives of aging Boomers confronting the flab of middle age and facing the fact that "gravity is reality." In response, Levi's created Dockers, a cotton twill pant for "maturing" Boomer men. Jeans manufacturers also moved away from an excruciatingly tight fit to very baggy, "anti-fit" pants. Since most mature Boomers can't shoehorn their way into 501s anymore, denim companies such as Lee, Wrangler, Levi Strauss, and Gitano have come to the rescue with roomier, body-friendly jeans.

Recreational risks. In the past seven years, orthopedic surgeons have seen a rise in the number of patients seeking treatment for knee problems—a 17 percent increase between 1985 and 1992. The reasons are varied but include the aging of Boomers. "We see a lot of knee injuries to baby boomers who want to act twenty-one but are actually fifty-one," says Dr. Paul A. Lotke, a professor of orthopedic surgery at the University of Pennsylvania Hospital in Philadelphia. "That younger generational self-image exposes people to more recreational risks."[9] Aging Boomers are gradually shifting to more sedate sports such as golf but a significant number continue to pursue rigorous physical activity to combat the ravages of time.

The eyes have it. Like it or not, Boomers' eyes are getting weaker. A common complaint among Boomers in the late 1990s is with small print, glare, and low-contrast color schemes. They are also more prone to eye diseases that commonly strike people in their forties and fifties. Glaucoma and presbyopia (farsightedness) mean eyedrops and bifocals can't be far away.

Other Signs

Changing interests. Young American players like tennis ace Andre Agassi are expected to dominate the future of tennis. "But in the long-term battle for aging baby boomer bodies and wallets, the game of Fred Couples will be the king of the swing." Says Thomas B. Doyle, of the National Sporting Goods Association, a trade group, "The demographics are favorable for golf." The number of golfers grew 22 percent from 1987 through 1991, and Doyle expects a steady 4 percent growth annually. Senior baby boomers are entering their mid-forties, the average age of golfers, and more of them will hit the links as their children get older. Boasts Church Yash, chairman of the National Golf Association: "A lot of people are getting out of tennis and into golf."[10]

Career frustration. Twenty years ago, midlife crisis most often referred to relationships. Now, the crisis revolves around careers. By the time most people reach middle age, they may have become successful in their careers, but the job that was once satisfying might have become depressingly routine. Career dissatisfaction is a typical midlife issue of the late 1990s. Mergers and downsizing have left many older Boomers feeling shut out and burnt out.

Okay, it's true. Boomers are getting older. Many spent the last decade getting into shape. They will spend the next decade coming to terms with the inevitable deterioration of their physical abilities. Age may be difficult to deal with. The passing years cannot be wished away. Yet all is not lost for the generation that rewrote the definitions of adolescence and youth. The middle adult years hold great challenge and promise. Stories like that of Norman Maclean, author of the much celebrated *A River Runs Through It and Other Stories*, testify to the fact that life is not over at fifty. Reaching this milestone in life stirs something in even the most successful Boomer; a sense of time, of last chances, of fresh starts, of responsibility for one's parents as well as one's children, and for many the realization that they're the person everyone looks to in the family. Turning fifty seems to sound a wake-up call to this largest of all generations.

A Wake-Up Call

The "Yuppie's Prayer" is becoming a sentiment of the past.

> Now I lay me
> down to sleep.
> I pray my Cuisinart to keep.
> I pray my stocks are on the rise,
> and that my analyst is wise,
> that all the wine I sip is white
> and that my hot tub's watertight,
> that racquetball won't get too tough,
> that all my sushi's fresh enough.
> I pray my cordless phone still works,
> that my career won't lose its perks,
> my microwave won't radiate,
> my condo won't depreciate.
> I pray my health club doesn't close
> and that my money market grows.
> If I grow broke before I wake
> I pray my Volvo they won't take.
>
> Unknown

It's time to review the past, rethink the future, and figure out how to live—and stretch—the years ahead. One thing people do when they hit middle age is look at the life goals they haven't yet accomplished. They get a little greater sense of urgency. They tend to think more about what's left to do rather than what's done. "You have to come to grips with some wake-up calls, like you're not going to live forever," comments Ross Goldstein, a San Francisco psychologist who specializes in studying Boomers. "You realize that you're not going to become president of the company, leave alone the country." "The important thing is that those realizations are the beginning of chapters, not the ends," he continues. "What it means is that you accept that you can have a good life despite not having reached all your goals."[11]

Dr. Donna Webb, associate director of the Center for Lifelong Learning, Loma Linda University in Southern California, believes, "Today, baby boomers are taking positive steps toward developing congruent goals and lifestyles. They are creating a more balanced way of life, knowing that they can accomplish their dreams—but in stages, rather than all at once."[12]

Life in the Slow Lane

Many Boomers are finding that there is life after the rat race. Both "voluntary" and "involuntary" simplicity is being adopted by middle-aged adults. It's been called the new simplicity, downscaling, cashing out, and "America's fatigue with excess." After working too many hours during the day and trying to fit family and personal activities into the little time that is left over, Boomers are realizing that quality of life is determined by more than quantity of possessions. As a result, they are voluntarily cutting back on work to live simpler lifestyles. "When I'm seventy years old, I'm never going to look back and wish I had spent more time at my job," says Margie Dunki Jacobs, a Vermont mother who recently cut her family's income by about ten thousand dollars when she quit her part-time job to spend more time with her children. "Certainly the times you have with your family mean the most."[13] Admittedly the trend is still small, with only about 5 percent of all Americans practicing voluntary simplicity. The Trends Research

Institute in Rhinebeck, New York, predicts, however, that by the end of the decade 15 percent of all Boomers will be working less, earning less, and saving more.[14]

A portion of those embracing the new simplicity will do so involuntarily as layoffs and downsizing make it imperative. Lower wages will lead to an era of thrift, savings, and antimaterialism. This is a real benefit to overworked and stressed Boomers, many of whom are beginning to realize that they have been too materialistic. Targeted by advertisers almost as soon as they came out of the womb, Boomers have been made to believe that they need a lot of things. As they mature through midlife, many are seeing for the first time that the things they own are not making them happy. They are learning to enjoy things that don't require either money or fancy equipment, like watching a sunset, playing with the dog, or going for a walk.

Since 1985 Bersch and Company, of Century City, California, has licensed fourteen hit games—including Taboo, SongBurst, and Scrutineyes. The company "commissioned a marketing study that showed that baby boomers were rediscovering games as cheap home entertainment." Blame it on "cocooning" or the first signs of gray hair: Many Baby Boomers are spending their leisure time playing Pictionary and Scrabble.[15] "Baby boomers have money, they're sophisticated, and they're consuming less alcohol," says John Rohs, a restaurant analyst at Wertheim Schroder & Company. "Now, baby boomers can name-drop coffees such as Jamaican Blue Mountain instead of wines like Chateauneuf-du-Pape."[16]

A Poignant Searching

Midlife can be a testing time for marriages and relationships. Children may be off at college and careers may be winding down. "In our culture, being young is what is valued, being physically attractive," writes Diane Sanford, a St. Louis psychologist who works with women's midlife issues. "Women whose self-esteem has been tied up in looking sexy start to have a lot of difficulty dealing with the change. Women and men can give more importance to the qualities that don't change over time," Sanford suggests, "being caring, being smart, generous, a good friend. Those are the ways to preserve a relationship."[17]

Learning how to deal with anger, hostility, and stress is also high on the Boomers' checklist. Festering anger, hostility, and stress are key factors that will set Boomers up for a heart attack in middle adulthood. As individuals grow older, they often realize the need to straighten things out. This is likely to be an important theme as Boomers seek to patch up relationships with their parents. The 1950s and 1960s found parent/child relationships stretched beyond the breaking point for many. The middle adult years are ones in which real closeness between Boomers and their parents is possible. There is a poignant search for connection.

Downsizing Dreams

Downsizing and streamlining by employers means Boomer dreams of retiring early may need to be reworked. As of 1995 the average retirement age was around fifty-eight years old—two years younger than a decade ago and seven years earlier than what was long considered the typical "gold watch" age. Helping to lower the retirement age was cost-cutting accomplished by employers offering early-retirement packages. The trend, however, is already reversing. Many aging Boomers will have to work longer. Even though 55 percent of them hope to retire before age sixty-five, most will not have the financial wherewithal to do so.

Boomers feel bombarded by dire predictions about their chances for enjoying a comfortable retirement. Sixty-nine percent of Boomers fear not having enough money for retirement, 54 percent believe Social Security will collapse, 56 percent worry about losing their jobs, and 71 percent are concerned about maintaining their income.[18] The most pressing issue is the stability of Social Security. If Social Security benefits are reduced, as most analysts predict must happen, then Boomers will not enjoy the same level of retirement that current retirees do.

Boomers' financial outlook is not all bad. An astonishing national transfer of wealth is now under way. It is estimated that over the next ten years between seven and one hundred billion dollars will pass from one generation to another. This amounts to the greatest transfer of wealth in the history of our country. Thanks to post–World War II prosperity, the average net worth of U.S. households headed by persons sixty-five and up is $258,000, and the average inheritance they will leave their Boomer children is about $50,000.[19] The available data shows that the combined personal net worth of Americans over fifty-five is more than eight trillion, not including pensions and Social Security. The vast majority of that wealth will fall into the laps of Boomers. Never before have so many people been poised to inherit so much. Of course, it's an open question as to how much of this wealth will survive medical expenses and other ravages of old age.[20]

And, despite what you read, Boomers are saving more money for retirement than many perceive. According to Cheryl Russell, noted Boomer researcher, "Boomers are doing better than their parents because they have had fewer children and because baby-boom women are more likely to work than were their mothers."[21] A Merrill Lynch report concluded that Boomers are saving only about one-third of what they need for retirement. Russell reveals that the Lynch study didn't include housing wealth. Once housing wealth is calculated into the figures, Boomers are saving approximately 84 percent of what they need for retirement.

Growing Spiritual Openness

As the 60s and 70s unraveled, Boomers appeared to be absent from churches. And though this trend was no different from that followed by young people of other generations, the Boomer generation is larger than those before it, making the Boomers' absence more conspicuous. A Gallup research study throughout 1993 based on telephone interviews with representative nationwide samples of 3,829 men and women found that Boomers are statistically unremarkable, mirroring the religious characteristics of the general population. Summarizing their reports, George H. Gallup Jr. and Robert Bezilla assert that, ". . . it still must be said that there are a lot of baby boomers, and they are going to grow older and probably live longer than their parents. The older people get, the more religion becomes important to them and the more they tend to go to church; there is no reason to believe the baby boomers will be any different."[22]

A Spiritual Search

The recent best-seller by Stephen R. Covey, *The 7 Habits of Highly Effective People*,[23] demonstrates the desire people in America have for moral and spiritual direction. His message—stressing principles like kindness, integrity, honesty, patience, and loyalty—has struck a chord. More than six million copies of his book have been sold in North America alone, and it has been translated into twenty-eight languages. While Covey's ideas are not new, they are capturing the attention of millions of Americans who desire a return to "moral decency." Says Gerald Celente, who directs the Trends Research Institute, "There is a basic message that's not being taught at home or at school and is not being fostered in the workingplace." The nation, Celente notes, is spiritually adrift: "People are looking for direction. They're lost."[24]

Doing It Their Way

Generational studies have long pointed out that people going through transitional events—middle adulthood—are often open to the gospel of Christ. But Boomers are redesigning the typical search for spiritual depth to fit their own culture. For example, it is well-known that exercise videotapes have been popular with fitness-conscious Boomers. Since 1994 a genre has emerged that capitalizes on that popularity, seeking to meet the needs of those trying to improve their lives spiritually, as well as physically. Balancing physical and spiritual exercise, these videos instruct viewers in body, mind, and spirit. The trend caught fire in 1994 when yoga videos took off, capturing 5 percent of the exercise video market. Most of the current videos on the market will be found in the New Age fitness category of yoga and tai chi. Also to be found are videos with flying angels, hypnosis, and Native American teachings. While these videos are not acceptable to orthodox Christians, they do point out that, "Baby boomers are aging and facing their own mortality. Their children are growing up, and they're facing the big issues: 'Who am I? Why am I here? How do I live a harmonious life?'" says Al Cattabianai, president of Wellspring Media.[25] "It's not just some new age, metaphysical person anymore; it's everyone looking for meaning in their lives," says Paul Solomon, president of Distributor International Video Network.[26]

Yearning for Yesterday

Yesterday looms large in the minds of Boomers. In earlier generations nostalgia—a word coined in 1600 by a Swiss physician to describe homesickness—focused on specific places. Boomer mobility has changed the focus of nostalgia from places—home and farm—to celebrities, music, and films of the past. Because the material record of their nostalgia is in the archives of the media, the popularity of old films, commercials, and products is not surprising. The Boomers' current passion to relive the past is in large measure a response to the rapid pace of change in their lives. But even nostalgia has its own wake-up calls, as when Annette Funicello, whom many Boomer men had a crush on as boys during her Mouseketeer days, announced that she has multiple sclerosis. Or when Mickey Mantle succumbed to lung cancer in 1995.

Marketers center their appeals to nostalgia based on what was popular when Boom-

Twelve Reasons Boomers Return to Church

1. Boomers are concerned about the moral training of their children.

2. Boomers are questioning the meaning of their lives.

3. Boomers are nostalgic and wish to relive earlier times.

4. Boomers are seeking security from the rapid pace of change.

5. Boomers are frustrated at living less well than they had planned.

6. Boomers are anxious about society, the environment, and materialism.

7. Boomers are realizing that the answer is not in things but in a personal faith.

8. Boomers are looking for a lifestyle that is meaningful.

9. Boomers are pursuing a new balance by looking deeper into their lives.

10. Boomers are hunting new and meaningful experiences.

11. Boomers are coping with aging parents and still-young children.

12. Boomers are turning fifty and reaching a midlife malaise.

ers were twelve years old. Fred Davis, a professor at the University of California, San Diego, and the author of *Yearning for Yesterday: A Sociology of Nostalgia,* remarks that "We turn to the past for psychological security and comfort, which present times deny us."[27] Part of the openness to a spiritual search by Boomers can be directly tied to their nostalgia. Many Boomers were attending church when they were twelve years old. The heights of church membership and attendance were achieved in the 1950s and early 1960s, when Boomers were children. "In fact, more than four out of five Boomers were raised with a religious background. . . ."[28]

The Yuppie Is Dead

Another indication that Boomers are changing their approach to life is seen in the way they buy products. In the 1980s as Boomers tried to define their identity, they often went on buying binges, consuming products in such haste that they were labeled the "Me Generation," and the 80s became known as the "Me Decade." Now most Boomers no longer need such superficial badges of identity. Their aging has developed a more sober, thrifty, family-oriented generation. "America's new grown-ups" realize that the extravagant Yuppie days of wine and roses are officially over. As they've aged, their emphasis has shifted from the quantity of possessions to the quality of life—a natural result of progression into middle adulthood. Their desire for quality of life transfers into a desire for depth and spiritual renewal. "Historically, rebellious and self-centered generations like the baby boomers, however much resented in their younger years, have tended to age well and to be appreciated eventually for their wisdom."[29]

Slowing for God?

The Boomers are turning fifty, but that doesn't mean they're slowing down. Boomers are still the independent, self-absorbed generation they've always been. As ever they remain obsessed with their own agendas. It's only their focus that has changed. In the 60s and 70s they focused on antiwar protests, civil rights, and legalizing marijuana. As they begin to move through middle age, they now focus on finding time for family, restoring lost relationships, and saving for retirement.

So what does this mean for the church? As always, Boomers will keep changing the ground rules. Boomers are just hitting their stride. More than ever, they are calling the shots in government, business, and churches. Boomer power is the top 1996 trend according to the Trends Research Institute.[30]

A hopeful trend in the late 1980s and early 1990s was reported by CNN, *USA Today*, the *Wall Street Journal*, and other popular sources of information.

A number of studies claimed that Boomers were coming back to church.[31] The main reason for their return? They desired religious education for their own children. And it was true: between 1987 and 1991 Boomers did return to churches in a major way. In part their return was sparked by the start of the Gulf War in January of 1991. Church attendance typically goes up with the outbreak of a war, and the trend held true for the first part of 1991. But the period of Boomer return may be reversing, according to David Roozen of Hartford Seminary in a new study, "Empty Nest, Empty Pew: The Boomers Continue Through the Life Cycle."[32] In analyzing worship attendance data from the National Opinion Research Center at the University of Chicago, Roozen found that when their children reach their teens, older Boomers actually go to church less often. "Early research shows even baby boomer parents, who returned to worship with their young children, are fading away from churches as their kids become too-busy teens," says Roozen.[33]

They become even less active in church when their children eventually leave home. Thus the leading edge (born 1946–1954) of the generation is most likely to have already returned to church and may be thinking of leaving again as they face the empty nest. However, the trailing edge (born 1954–1964) of the generation may be coming back to church since they are more likely to still have children at home.

Why do returning Boomers leave when they face the empty nest? George Barna, director of Barna Research Group, suggests, "Being rational people . . . Boomers also constantly analyze their environment and compare the benefits received against the costs incurred. After a few years of gathering the information necessary to draw a conclusion, the verdict is now in. The Church is guilty of irrelevance. Kids or no kids, literally hundreds of thousands of Boomers are exiting."[34]

However, it's more complex than that. The strongest predictor of church involvement among Boomers is whether they have young children at home. Unpredictable parenting cycles among Boomers mean some older, leading-edge Boomers may still fit that predictor, i.e., have younger children at home. Some Boomers find themselves in a strange position on life's timeline—able to take advantage of over-fifty discounts and children's discounts at the same time. In 1975 only 5 percent of first births nationwide were to women over age thirty, according to the National Center on Health Statistics. In 1988 the percentage jumped to 17 percent. The increase of second marriages and the delaying of children have fueled the phenomenon of the older parent.

Beyond having younger children at home, one has to take into consideration the total life cycle, which, as it progresses, has a settling down quality. As people age they tend to desire a stronger faith, settle into a church, and make few major changes. As people reach fifty, they tend to become more reflective and review the past. The following confession appeared in *Toronto Life* magazine under the title, "The Baby Boom Blues." It's a startling account of facing reality, a reality that drives many Boomers on a continuing spiritual search.

> I grew up in a generation that was headstrong, outspoken, arrogant, brazen, impatient, self-righteous and fiercely idealistic. It was a promising time: there were many who expected us to transform our world, and I think in many ways we did. . . . What we accomplished was astounding and good. If, at times, we lacked a sense of balance, we more than compensated with passion.
>
> I find myself gazing wistfully over my shoulder a lot these days. My contemporaries were galvanized by the sense of purpose people feel when they embrace a collective vision, when they are inspired by touchstones outside themselves and have faith in the future.

But I look around me now, and what I see troubles me: my generation has lost its moral bearings, there is only disenchantment; where once there was community, there is only rootlessness.

I cannot have a conversation these days without feeling uneasy. My contemporaries are restless. Something is wrong. Far too many people, it seems to me, are disappointed. Everybody's looking for something, but no one is certain how to find it.

"What's wrong with our generation?" I wonder aloud. "Why is everybody so screwed up? . . . Because we thought we could have it all, and then we did have it all, and we found out it was nothing."[35]

The history of Boomers records how they challenged every American institution. Beginning with protests to secure greater civil rights for Black Americans in the 50s, Boomers protested the war in Vietnam; refused to buy grapes grown in California; experimented with drugs; burned bras; and explored alternative religions. Hare Krishnas set up shop in airports, gurus established ashrams, Moonies and Jesus freaks vied for new converts, and Aquarians proclaimed the dawning of a "New Age." Their lifelong search for a spiritual base is only now maturing.

As they age, millions are, or will be, seeking a sense of spiritual connection, a place of worship. Churches have a chance for growth and resurgence during the last half of the 1990s by reaching out to these aging Boomers but only if they become (1) less stodgy and flexible enough to meet the real personal needs of Boomers who come to them, (2) sensitive to the needs of Boomers in areas outside of traditional spiritual concerns, (3) adaptable to giving Boomers a wide variety of participational choices, (4) responsive to the musical styles and tastes of Boomers, and (5) assertive in challenging Boomers to a great vision.

3

Generation X-Cellent

Suddenly Busters are being noticed. After years of being hidden in the shadows of the larger Boomer generation, it seems that everyone is targeting this youthful generation. Countless books and articles struggle to come to terms with this thirteenth generation since America's independence. Unfortunately very few organizations—from Madison Avenue marketers to religious organizations—are hitting the mark. Researchers are beginning to discover that many of the characteristics they attributed to Busters are not holding up. *Newsweek* recently confessed, "There are only two generalizations we can make about them with any degree of certainty: they are Americans, and they are in their 20s."[1]

While some of the earliest speculations about Busters have not been proven, there still remain a few broad characteristics that appear to be holding firm.

Characteristics of Busters

The children of the Boomers—a.k.a. Busters—are a new breed. They think differently, their values are different, and their needs are different. For sure they are not younger versions of the Boomers. One thing we know, the Buster generation resents being stereotyped as a homogeneous target market. This younger generation has a hard time being labeled and they particularly dislike being referred to as Generation X. In fact the label "Generation X" was chosen by only 10 percent of Busters surveyed in a recent poll.[2] Busters feel that they have inherited a world of chaos, environmental destruction, wrecked families, AIDS, unemployment, and a huge deficit that they didn't create. Having endured family breakups, Busters have either grown up dysfunctional or have learned to adapt to change and ambiguity very well. Relationships between Busters and their parents are generally better than those between Boomers and their parents. There is less of a generation gap between the Busters and the Boomers.

Compared to their parents' generation, the size of this generation is small. After the record number of Boomer births, anything less seemed like a "bust." But let's not forget that Busters are the second largest population group in United States history. They represent a group larger than the entire population of Canada and account for about one-fifth of the adult population in the United States. Depending on how one brackets this generation, nearly forty-one million twenty to thirty-one-year-olds in 1997 are becoming the hottest demographic group in our nation. The Boomlet—twenty-five million thirteen to nineteen-year-olds—is trailing them.[3] Together this "bust" generation comprises a whopping sixty-six million individuals!

Eclectic Tastes in Music

Being the most diverse generation in U.S. history, Busters are too different to catalog with a one-size-fits-all analysis. They are a fragmented group not easy to pigeonhole. Their fragmentation can be seen in the lack of teen idols. In the history of teen stardom, including Frank Sinatra, Elvis Presley, and The Beatles, the teen idols who have become icons have all been musical. In the Buster generation, music has become so polarized, it's hard for any one person to gain teen stardom. Radio has so diversified—with Top 40 stations giving way to alternative music, classic rock, hard rock, rap, and country stations—that one form of music doesn't gather enough followership to create teen idols. MTV reflects this fragmentation in its programing, which runs the gamut from rap to R & B to alternative to pop music. Consider the recent return to popularity of Tony Bennett. Beginning with an innocent parody of "New York, New York" on *The Simpsons* T.V. show, Bennett moved on to record an *MTV Unplugged* special with the likes of k.d. lang, Lemonhead Evan Dando, and other pop and rock musicians. "Bennettmania" pushed the album version of the *Unplugged* special to the top of the *Billboard* jazz charts and to number sixty-nine on the pop charts. Tony Bennett as a Buster idol? It's yet another example of the difficulty of targeting the fragmented Buster generation.

Concern for the Environment

While even the oldest Busters don't remember much about April 22, 1970—the first Earth Day—throughout their lifetime, environmental events have united them in a common effort to protect the environment. Defining events that occurred in their formative years include the formation of the Environmental Protection Agency (1970), banning of DDT (1972), Endangered Species Act (1973), Safe Drinking Water Act (1974), Three Mile Island near-meltdown (1979), Superfund law to clean up toxic dumps (1980), ozone hole discovered over Antarctic (1985), Chernobyl nuclear meltdown (1985), Exxon Valdez crude oil leak (1989), California Desert Protection Act (1994), and gray wolves reintroduced into Yellowstone National Park (1995). Over the twenty-seven years since the first Earth Day, much progress has been made, with air pollution down more than 25 percent. In 1972 only 36 percent of all the rivers and lakes in the United States were clean, but by 1992 nearly 62 percent were fishable and swimmable.

Familiar with Technology

Coming of age in the uproar of the information age, the Busters live in a world of computers, gigabytes, and cyberspace. They were raised on *Sesame Street* and in *Mr. Rogers' Neighborhood*. They travel the information superhighway with ease. They are at home with infotainment, video, and soundbites. Cyberspace defines the way they choose to participate in the world—fun and fast. Influenced even more profoundly by technology than the Boomers, they prefer a stimulating and varied environment. Busters caught on quickly to technology because they spent a lot of time with electronic devices as children. Just as earlier generations spent time with cars, Busters spent time with technology. They browse the electronic landscape like pros. Busters push the envelope of communication toward interactivity. Involvement in the process and medium is expected. They understand being "wired" and are already heavily immersed in computers where they control their actions and involvement.

Nostalgic

Nostalgia is not exclusive to the Boomers. Busters too are getting sentimental over the 1980s and harkening back to their childhoods. The decade is revived with tributes to the rock group Duran Duran, leg warmers, and the T.V. show *Dynasty.* It's the first nostalgia movement to be claimed by the Busters. Time seems to have sped up so much that even events that occurred just a few years ago are viewed with a certain sentimentality.

Activists

In the 1990s eighteen- to twenty-nine-year-olds are twice as likely to participate in organized demonstrations as Boomers were. The face of Washington, D.C., is being transformed by Buster activists, who are part of the first administration whose chief not only remembers where he was when John F. Kennedy was shot but also where he was when John Lennon was killed. This generation is much more individualistic than the Boomers ever were. They believe they can control their own destiny; make themselves do whatever is possible; make themselves become whatever they long to be. They want to serve in organizations that tolerate a broader personal style. Their skills include computer literacy, an understanding of diversity, and a global mind-set. They want to serve where they can get satisfaction from their involvement. You might say they are "constructively rebellious." They get things done but not necessarily the way others expect them to. They would rather be where the action is than climb the traditional ladder of success. Adaptability and energy are their strong points. They are frustrated by predictability and lack of continual progress. They thrive in a creative, dynamic environment where they enjoy work and are evaluated on what they actually accomplish rather than the style of their dress.

What Are Busters Searching For?

Busters are a generation in search of an identity. Emerging information suggests that Busters yearn for more traditional structures. Leaders would be wise to take note of this change, but not to read it as a renaissance of the 1950s. As with all cyclical events in history, there is a backlash. If they sense that a ministry is tailored for Boomers, they'll reject it because they tend to reject anything that Boomers like or accept. Busters want to define things on their own terms. So the challenge is to determine how to address the concerns and issues of their hearts. Since they don't know exactly who they are, addressing their needs is difficult.

Searching for Family

When all is considered, Busters are longing for a sense of family. "What Generation Xers want, is a place to belong," suggests church consultant Robert Logan. "They have not been as well connected in their families, and they have a higher percentage of fragmented families or virtual absentee parents through work."[4] More Busters grew up in single-parent homes than members of any previous generation. Fifty percent of their parents were divorced or separated. This experience creates some disillusionment with relationships, which in turn leads to cynicism and reluctance to make the commitment of marriage. When they do marry, however, they take the institution and parenthood seriously.

Chynna Phillips, formerly with the pop group Wilson Phillips, is a classic example. Phillips literally had a Mama and a Papa for parents—John and Michelle Phillips of the famous singing group the Mamas and the Papas. She grew up in a fast-paced world with opportunities for travel, friends, and creativity. But her parents' experimentation with drugs and the pressures of fame left her part of a broken home when her parents split up when she was just two. In a recent article Chynna explained, "I want to be able to give my children what I didn't have. I want them to be able to feel a sense of family and commitment. My career will not be my first priority. I won't record if it takes too much time away from my kids."[5]

As children Busters generally had greater firsthand experience with crime than other generations, which contributes to their desire to look out for themselves. Busters want security, a home, and to be married. For example, in a 1990 Yankelovich Clancy Shulman poll, 64 percent of men and women aged eighteen to twenty-nine said they wanted to spend more time with their own children than their parents had spent with them.[6] Buster women, having observed the sacrifices made by many women in the 1960s and 1970s, seem determined to find a middle ground between feminism and traditionalism. Busters "prefer careers that are more than just financially rewarding and provide the flexibility to enjoy family and leisure time," notes Marian Selzman, president of BKG Youth in New York City. Says Stacey Steinmetz, a graduate of the University of Vermont, "Since I'm not going to make a lot of money anyway, I might as well get a job that rewards me in other ways, where I don't have to work long hours to get ahead."[7]

Searching for Peace

They are looking for anything that will help them get along better in our world. This includes healthy food, smaller starter homes, and even furnishings that fit a single lifestyle. Products or services that help them stay in touch attract their attention. Car phones, beepers, pagers, answering machines, E-mail, and fax machines are considered necessities. They don't like organizations to patronize them or condescend to them. Busters appreciate an education, especially one that helps them find a job. They will continue to be interested in job-related training and, as they age, open to spiritual instruction. They are most receptive to education that is presented through multimedia avenues such as video and computer rather than books. They are careful about spending money. Many are practicing Yankee thrift—don't buy it unless you need it, don't buy it new if used will do, and don't buy it at all if you have to use credit. They don't trust the system. Jobs are scarce, the interest on student loans is high, and the economy looks bleak. Few Busters feel confident enough to buy on credit.

Searching for Control

For Busters the key word is "control." They like to control their environment. Channel surfing, cruising the internet, and programing their CD player all allow them to exert a measure of the control they crave.

Contrary to popular opinion, Busters do not have a short attention span. Their love of the quick-cut, quick-fade format of television allows them to review whole segments of information at their own control. Channel surfing to Busters is the equivalent of skimming a book to older generations. They search, with remote control in hand, among varied options for whatever suits their tastes. Busters are able to process information from several sources quickly. Thus they rewind, re-view, talk on the phone, and do other chores all at the same time. Their mind responds to whatever information holds their attention. If the medium does not involve them, they quickly discard it in favor of more fruitful pursuits.

Attracting Busters to Church

At first glance Busters may appear to be less oriented to religion than former generations, but a comparison with the young adults of a decade ago finds little difference. *Emerging Trends,* published by the Princeton Religion Research Center, notes that, "The only noticeable difference between the generations is in the expression of religious preference."[8] The report indicates that Busters' affiliation with dominant religious groups such as Protestants, Roman Catholics, and Jews has declined while their participation in other religious groups has risen. *Emerging Trends* concludes,

> These findings suggest that, like generations before them, as the baby buster generation matures, its sense of importance of religion will increase, as will participation in membership in the church and frequent attendance of worship services. *What remains to be seen is whether the major faiths and denominations can attract young adult members* who will identify themselves with a specific denomination or set of beliefs (italics mine).[9]

It is true that as a group Busters have ignored churches. Dr. Charles Arn, president of Church Growth, Inc., in Monrovia, California, lists four attitudes Busters have toward the traditional church.

1. *They see it as boring.* Sitting in a pew for an hour requires a program that retains their interest, moves rapidly, and involves them in the process. Their image of the traditional church includes none of these.
2. *They perceive it to be irrelevant.* The things that worry these young adults, the problems they struggle with, the successes they seek on a daily basis must be addressed in church, or it is perceived as a waste of time.
3. *They have other things they would rather be doing.* Time is one of their most treasured possessions. Recreation, socializing, and investment in one's own betterment receive a priority of any spare time available.
4. *They feel that no one attending will be like them.* Busters are looking for others like themselves for a verification that there is something there worth going for.[10]

Social commentators often depict Busters as rootless, shunning tradition, and searching for a sense of identity. Much of this is true, of course, but not really much different than other generations at the same age. The Busters are coming of age and a new round of changes is on the way. As a generation they are finding their voice. They have grown up with traumatic changes rocking their world and most are thriving in the new landscape that is emerging. Poised to claim some of the power that has been held so long by the Boomers, they are ready to take responsibility for things that are important to them.

Busters are a much wiser generation than they are often given credit for. When they were children, Busters learned never to take the media at face value. They learned to be critical and to recognize hype. Disappointment with ads they saw as children led them to approach media hype with caution and skepticism. Due to their latchkey childhood, which left many of them to fend for themselves, Busters are an extremely savvy group. They have developed a hardened cynical edge, which makes it more difficult to attract them. While they are not antiadvertising, they do dislike insincerity. Advertising cannot be misleading, offensive, or boring. They have little difficulty seeing through hype.

Thus the hardest aspect of reaching Busters is learning how to approach them. In general, Busters will respond warmly to appeals that don't appear to target them specifically. The hard sell is definitely the wrong approach. They won't respond to it. Any hint of commercialism creates an extremely negative reaction. Our role as churches in the years beyond the turn of the century will be to find ways to communicate the gospel to Busters without assuming we can intrude on a passive audience. Busters want the gospel message but they want to exert some measure of control over how and when it is received. In addition, they are not going to be attracted to any church that seems more geared to their parents' needs and interests than to theirs.

Many Busters are disenchanted with the media hype and T.V. fads. They are looking for something real, something

Insights for Reaching Busters

1. Busters will attend churches that have a clear focus, narrowly defined vision, and assertive commitment to accomplish their mission.

2. Busters will attend churches where worship services are shorter, well designed, and have good flow and tempo.

3. Busters will attend churches that have a loud, upbeat, faster pop music sound.

4. Busters will attend churches that win their loyalty every Sunday through excellent ministry.

5. Busters will attend churches that focus on local ministry rather than on ministry in faraway places.

6. Busters will give money to churches where they can see their money achieving results.

7. Busters will volunteer for ministry activities that are short-term.

8. Busters will volunteer and minister to confront practical issues in their community.

9. Busters will attend churches that help them sort out the hurts in their lives through practical messages, classes, and small groups.

10. Busters will come to Christ through need-based ministries that deal with the hurts and internal issues they are facing.[11]

with substance that isn't laminated or plastic. They desire relationships and answers to the real questions of life. Their music—rap and alternative—is grounded in harsh realities: broken families, diminished financial expectations, contempt for society's institutions, gun control, single-parent families, rape. Therefore many Busters are searching for meaning in a world filled with contradictions and uncertainties. They are looking for that key something that will serve as an authority in their lives. Trend watcher John Naisbitt predicts that, "During turbulent times many people need a structure—not ambiguity—in their lives. They need something to hang on to, not something to debate. The demand for structure will increase."[12]

The bottom line? They're looking for honesty. Over the years they've seen how glorious promises have gone unfulfilled, whether it was their parents getting divorced or a promising economy going downhill. Busters don't want "perfect" Christians or overblown promises about the future. What they do seek is the plain, straightforward truth from churches and Christians who will admit to struggles, defeats, and real answers in response to their faith.

Busters are seeking relevance. An old story tells of a little girl who was afraid to go to sleep in the dark. One particularly difficult evening, her mother entered the bedroom several times to reassure the child. Each time her comforting words ended with the phrase, "God will take care of you." That thought didn't seem to make much of an impression on the tiny girl, alone in the large, dark bedroom. As her mother departed a last time, the small child wailed, "But, Mommy, I want God with a face." Busters want God with a face, and it must be the human face of a teacher, friend, coworker, family member, pastor, youth leader, or anyone who will take the time to coach them through the difficult issues in their lives.

Why try to reach out to them? Because they are the future. If you ignore the Busters, who make up about 30 percent of the United States population over thirteen years old, your church will be fishing in only 70 percent of the lake. Churches will dramatically begin to change as they reach the Buster generation. Busters will help control and lead churches in the next few decades. This element is crucial to understand as leaders face the future. A church that does not reach Busters may be in danger of dying.

Busters are open to church and spiritual issues, but a church filled with Busters must expect change and new approaches to ministry. In the majority of cases, it will take the development of new church models to reach a significant number of Busters.

4

The Choice of a New Generation

Nearly two thousand years ago, Jesus directed his disciples' attention to a group of people approaching them and declared, "Look on the fields, that they are white for harvest" (John 4:35). These challenging words still ring true in our world today. As outlined in the previous two chapters, Boomers and Busters are open to the gospel of Jesus Christ and will participate in local churches, *if* they are approached properly.

Boomers and Busters are "white for harvest," yet most of them, at least two-thirds, cannot be reached in the same way that the older Builder generation was reached. It may surprise you that many existing churches will have great difficulty in reaching the Boomer and Buster generations. However, the rapid pace of change over the years has meant that the generations under fifty are quite different from the older generation. A good example of these differences can be seen in television-watching habits. In their article, "The Generation X Difference," writers Nicholas Zill and John Robinson report that, "The big difference in television-viewing patterns is found not between busters and boomers, but between adults under age 50 and those aged 50 and older."[1]

The differences between those over fifty and those under fifty were recently pointed out by the Center for Retailing Studies, Texas A&M University.

Remember that people born after you aren't reacting the same way you are to many things. If you need to do some homework, just remember that:

- Twenty-two percent of customers don't remember the American Bicentennial Celebration.

- Thirty-three percent of the people living in the United States feel people have always been on the moon.
- Fifty percent are too young to remember the assassination of John F. Kennedy.
- Sixty-six percent are not old enough to remember the Korean War.
- Seventy percent don't remember "before T.V."
- Eighty-five percent are not old enough to remember the 1929 stock market crash.

The point: Customers are changing. And people who want to serve them have to change too.[2]

Over a decade ago, Gene Getz reminded church leaders that, "The twentieth-century church, then, must not ignore culture. If we do, we are neglecting a significant factor in formulating a philosophy of ministry that is truly biblical, and a contemporary strategy that is relevant, practical, and workable."[3] More recently George Barna reminded us, "We need to be Scripturally accurate, but culturally sensitive. In other words, we have something unchanging to give people; but the way we give it to them may change."[4]

As we seek to fulfill Christ's command to "make disciples of all the nations," we must take advantage of new church models that are effective in today's culture.

Focus on Your Target

It's no surprise that marketing experts target their advertisements to specific audiences. Pepsi's slogan, "Choice of a New Generation," was aimed directly at the Boomers. It was only the tip of the proverbial iceberg. Note this respectable list of companies who targeted Boomers in the 1980s.

Merrill Lynch, watching its clients age, formed a thirty-person "Emerging Investor Business nit" to attract the Boomers' dollar.

Nabisco Brands used to advertise Wheat Thins as crackers. Nabisco discovered a core of upscale Boomer customers and decided to market Wheat Thins as a health snack.

Mortgage lenders offered fifteen-year, fixed-rate mortgages to two-salary Baby-Boomer couples who could handle higher payments.

VF Corp, maker of Lee Jeans, introduced VF Jeans aimed at Boomers who desired quality.

Longines, the midscale watchmaker, developed what is "perhaps the most accurate wristwatch in the world." Why? To reach the Boomer market.

The National Livestock and Meat Board found that a third of all shoppers were either "active lifestyle" or "health-oriented" types. Since many of these customers were no doubt Boomers, it developed a "Meat Nutrifacts" promotional campaign to reach them.

Chevrolet hit one of the hottest campaigns in years. "The Heartbeat of America" ads enjoyed the same success as the "See the USA in your Chevrolet" campaign of the 1950s and 1960s.

McDonald's introduced "Mac Tonight" in an effort to target the Boomers who no longer found Ronald McDonald appealing.

Targeting specific people for sales purposes remains a popular advertising strategy as the Boomers enter middle adulthood and the Busters come of age. Ford Motor Company began building its new Mark VIII luxury coupe to compete for the dollars of affluent Boomers. Chevrolet is using spokespersons in their twenties in hopes of persuading Busters to buy its cars. NutraSweet uses Busters in its ads to attract them to try its sugar substitute.

An associate editor of *Leadership*, Mark Galli, reported in a 1991 issue that his search for common methodologies among successful churches resulted in a baffling variety. The only clear principle he found was that "each church I examined has decided that it cannot be all things to all people. In one way or another, each has decided its unique identity as well as whom it is able to reach."[5] The new models of church ministry that are being formed today do not ignore

Christ's call to go into all the world (Matt. 28:19); they just attempt to use their limited resources carefully. They know that having a clear priority will assist them in designing outreach and programing that will produce better results. "Instead of pretending they exist to serve everyone," writes Lyle Schaller, "these churches have carved out a specialized niche in ministry and seek to excel in that specialized role."[6] Schaller continues, "Evangelism in the nineties is niche. You pick out a segment, a slice of the market you want to try to reach, and develop a ministry for that slice."[7]

To reach people in our media-saturated world, it is crucial to select a target group, isolate it, and communicate to it. Churches that try to be all things to all people often end up being nothing to everyone. The real challenge today is how to get the right mix of old and new values in the message. Television networks try to find the right mix. Which of the following T.V. programs do you think would attract Busters, Boomers, and Builders?

Murphy Brown
Home Improvement
Murder She Wrote
Seinfeld
Friends
The Price Is Right

The answers are: Busters—*Seinfeld* and *Friends,* Boomers—*Murphy Brown* and *Home Improvement,* Builders—*Murder She Wrote* and *The Price Is Right.* In a similar manner churches have always targeted people with age-graded Sunday school, youth groups, and adult programing. The difference is that today it is equally important to target people as an evangelism strategy for the entire church ministry.

We Christians reject T.V. as a foundational resource for developing a strategy to reach people for Christ. And we are correct in doing so. We clearly do not get our directions from Hollywood. However, a few church leaders object to targeting specific people groups at all. They submit that first of all, the Good News is for all people, and any attempt to direct outreach to a specific segment of the population is contrary to the spirit of the New Testament. Second, God will send whom he will send; therefore, targeting is unnecessary since the sovereignty of God controls all. Third, while resources can be focused on specific areas such as youth programs or a new housing tract, as far as the larger church ministry is concerned, there is limited value in targeting people.

As with most criticism, there are elements of truth in each of these objections to targeting. We should ask, however, "What was the strategy of Jesus?" Or even more broadly, "What was the strategy of God throughout the ages to reach the world?" While this book is not intended to be a theological treatise on targeting specific groups of people, it seems quite clear that the strategy of targeting specific people groups has been God's way to reach the world. After Adam and Eve rebelled against God as recorded in Genesis 3, God made what most believe is the first promise of a redeemer in verse 15: "And I will put enmity between you and the woman, and between your seed and her seed; He shall bruise you on the head, and you shall bruise him on the heel." Now, exactly how did God go about bringing his Son, the Redeemer of the world, into the world? He targeted a single family, that of Abram. It was through this single family that God promised the Savior when he said, "And in you all the families of the earth shall be blessed" (Gen. 12:3).

Jesus obviously came to earth to be the Savior of all people. Yet his strategy was similar to that found throughout the Old Testament. He carefully targeted an initial group of people whom he trained to carry on his work after his ascension. He chose twelve men, and all but one of them were Galileans (see Acts 2:7)! The fact is Jesus did not try to reach the entire world of various people groups at one time. His strategy was to target a specific audience through whom his message could be delivered to other audiences.

How then are we to reach our community or city or state or nation or world for Christ? By beginning with a clear target! Martin Marty reminds us that, "An advertisement or a sign that says 'Everyone Welcome' is useless. Who is everyone? People must be beckoned and invited personally."[8] To be certain, our responsibility is to "make disciples of all the nations," but we must do so one target at a time. The Great Commission even embodies this understanding in the word "nations," which properly means "peoples" or more precisely "people groups" such as clans, tribes, and castes. Jesus inherently knew that a local church would be effective in reaching only a limited number of people. In order for them to do so, they would need to target a specific subset of the population either intentionally or unintentionally.

Put the Hymnbooks Away

As we approach a new millennium, we must begin to distinguish between what are merely our traditions and what are the fundamental biblical truths that are shaping the future of the church. "One of the most tragic consequences of culture change is that some Christians cannot emotionally tolerate a variance in lifestyles because they have come to equate certain eternalities with being biblical."[9] To reach Boomers and Busters, our churches will have to exhibit a spirit of openness and graciousness that allows for the development of new styles of ministry. Unfortunately, churches are viewed by Boomers and Busters as outdated. To many people under fifty years old, churches are bastions of unchangeable people and ideas. This is recognized by John Stott who notes, "as for churches, many have a preponderance of the middle-aged and elderly, who have grown out of the protest phase and can be relied on to be comparatively docile. . . . however, the young vote with their feet and steer clear of such archaic institutions."[10]

Individually Boomers and Busters have their differences. Yet these two generations have enough similarities to constitute a group that has unique implications for churches seeking to reach them in the coming years. Boomers and Busters are receptive to the gospel and local churches. They are seeking meaning for life at their unique life stages. Studies show that they respond to ministries with vision, passion, and values. Yet they are quite skeptical about the institutional church. In particular they distrust the bureaucracy and fiscal irresponsibility they perceive attached to it. "To counteract this perception," suggests Dr. Kent Hunter, director of the Church Growth Center in Corunna, Indiana, "the local church should show a high regard for fiscal responsibility and a low profile for organization, politics, voting, and business meetings."[11]

Boomers and Busters appreciate options and choices. They have grown up in a Baskin-Robbins-31-Flavors world. Churches hoping to attract them must provide choices in worship times, styles, and days of the week. Varied opportunities must also be made available for ministry, training, and spiritual growth. Churches must remain sensitive to the fact that Boomers and Busters have grown accustomed to switching channels with the touch of the remote control if what they are watching fails to keep their interest. Thus they will not hesitate to switch churches that do not speak to their heart issues in ways that honestly communicate the truth of God's Word.

Boomers and Busters socialize primarily through the workplace and in units of friends. Effective evangelism in our era will take place through personal friendships and need-oriented workshops, small groups, and classes. Churches that tend to do outreach only through traditional programs will likely decline. Growing churches must train their people to share their faith among friends, family, neighbors, and workers.

Boomers and Busters are part of a high-tech, high-touch world. They will have fewer friends, but those they have will be like family. Larger group meetings that focus primarily on fellowship will continue to be difficult to start and maintain. Smaller groups that focus on specific projects or issues will continue to grow. As an outgrowth of their need orientation, both Boomers and Busters will gravitate to churches that meet their felt needs. Denominational names will mean less than the church's perceived ability to touch their hearts.

Symbolism is important to Boomers and Busters, due to their visual orientation. Preaching in the last half of the 1990s must include dialogue, parables, and visuals such as video or skits. Communicating a church's vision and mission in descriptive terms that paint a picture of the future is necessary to attract Boomers and Busters to a church.

All of these ideas reflect the importance of viewing the unchurched community as a mosaic of people groups. Once a church identifies its target groups, it can develop a strategy to reach them. By designing strategies that are sensitive to the specific needs and interests of its target group or groups, we will turn the complexity of the community into an opportunity for ministry. While it is difficult to generalize too much, it is agreed by most of those who study Boomers and Busters that a mixture of the following points should be employed in order to reach these generations.

1. *Develop new ministries.* There is a need for multiple ministry options to attract and hold Boomers and Busters. Some possible ministries to offer are divorce counseling; preschools and elementary schools; stepparenting and singles ministries; support groups for those combating drugs, alcoholism, homosexuality, and marital breakdowns; and marriage enrichment.

2. *Plan positive worship services.* Use contemporary music that stresses praise/worship. Allow participation through applause, the uplifting of hands, hugging, and other forms of personal involvement. Use media such as an overhead projector, films, videos, and dramas. Create movement and flow by building services around themes and eliminating dead spots. Only announce what is important for the entire congregation. Read Scripture from a modern translation and print high-quality bulletins and handouts. Don't neglect sin, but give people answers, not simply guilt. Raise the quality of worship. Use music that is relational and encourage conversation. Offer music on electronic instruments instead of traditional hymns played on an organ or piano. Since Boomers and Busters don't like choirs as much as singing the songs themselves, consider eliminating the choir or using it for special occasions.

3. *Stress lifestyle evangelism.* Don't force Boomers and Busters to evangelize by knocking on doors. Instead emphasize relationships, and encourage them to speak to their friends and family members. Use nonthreatening avenues such as parties, athletic events, and concerts. Redirect major events such as Valentine Banquets, Harvest Dinners, and Sunday school picnics toward the unchurched. Provide alternate ways to acknowledge acceptance of Christ, such as decision cards or after-service meetings in prayer rooms. Generally, Boomers and Busters do not like to be asked to come forward during the service.

4. *Provide quality child care.* Improve church nurseries with better lighting, newer carpets, new and clean toys, bright colors, open and accessible spaces, and well-baby policies. Structure programing along the lines of Jim Hensen's Muppets and include "Learning Centers" in Sunday school.

5. *Restructure existing services.* Make the evening service more than a "junior varsity" worship service by building in time for families. Develop classes around needs, use small groups, and move adult education to Sunday evenings or a weeknight. Experiment with worship services on Friday and Saturday evenings or early Sunday morning, as these tend to fit the Boomer and Buster lifestyle better than the traditional Sunday service.

6. *Offer opportunities for ministry.* Build ministry opportunities around relationships that stress spiritual gifts. Provide training and ask for shorter commitments—don't give "life sentences." Recruit through personal contact that emphasizes team ministry and plays down superstar ministry. Focus on building an army, not an audience.

7. *Plant new churches.* At least one hundred thousand new churches are needed in the United States to reach the Boomers and Busters. New churches often bring a new style of ministry that is attractive to these younger adults. They allow for the creation of new structures, are more open to incorporating new people, and create more vision and challenge than older churches.

8. *Upgrade facilities and equipment.* Provide clean and attractive facilities. Freshly stripe the parking lot and clear weeds and grass from cracks in sidewalks. Paint facilities, install glass entry doors for increased visibility and easy access, and improve lighting in auditoriums and classrooms. Modernize equipment by introducing computers, video cameras, and modern sound equipment. Don't skimp on the expenditures, since Boomers and Busters will take one look at poor equipment and never come back.

9. *Practice relational preaching.* Use solid content with real-life illustrations that Boomers and Busters face daily. Practice using illustrations that relate to women as well as men. Limit

preaching to twenty to thirty minutes. Stress practical living or "fix-it" sermons with messages that Boomers and Busters will find relevant to their everyday lives—how to avoid extramarital affairs, cope with job loss, or keep your kids off drugs.

10. *Make guests welcome.* Provide a welcome center that uses trained greeters to give a warm welcome to all guests. Provide welcome packets and make good use of directional signs that are up-to-date. Provide a fellowship time after worship for guests instead of members. Don't embarrass Boomers and Busters; welcome them from the pulpit without having them stand and speak. Encourage hugging, as Boomers and Busters like to experience warmth and closeness.

11. *Expect less formality.* Boomers and Busters have deeply rooted independent attitudes. They tend to avoid highly structured approaches to ministry. Use first names. Don't stress titles like "Rev." or "Dr." Encourage conversation and allow for casual dress, talking, and a relaxed atmosphere.

12. *Emphasize purpose and vision.* Build strong vision and stress the challenges and dreams your church hopes to accomplish. Require orientation classes (Pastor's Class or New Members' Class) for all new people. Build loyalty around the mission and vision of your church.

13. *Create opportunities for belonging.* Build on the desire for relationships and family by developing small groups. Use a combination of Bible studies, prayer groups, fellowship groups, social groups, task groups, accountability groups, and support groups. Reliance on one type of group, such as a Bible study group, will usually not work.

14. *Expand the roles of women.* Opportunities for women to be involved in ministry will vary from church to church. However, Boomers and Busters look for churches that take seriously the gifts, talents, calling, and proven ability of women to serve.

15. *Schedule fewer events.* Cluster several events together so people can have fewer nights out, and eliminate services or events that are becoming ineffective. Use weekend retreats, short seminars, and training events that do not ask for long-term attendance. Schedule with commuters and working women in mind.[12]

The unfortunate truth is that churches often ignore the changes that must be made to effectively reach Boomers and Busters. As Peter Drucker notes, "The only thing we know about the future is that it will be different."[13] Yet churches do not seem to be convinced it will be different. Even if it is different, we think, it won't be different for us! If our churches are to effectively reach Boomers and Busters, we will have to pay attention to what these generations are attracted to. This is not compromise! Rather it is doing what we can to understand the fields that must be harvested.

5

The Seeker-Centered Model

How do you share the "Old, Old Story" with young generations that have grown up in a high-tech, media-saturated, and fast-paced society? That was the question in the 1960s and 1970s in the United States as traditional churches took notice of declining attendance. Empty pews, older members, and fewer volunteers alerted churches to a Boomer drain. Today as we approach the twenty-first century, there is a corresponding Buster drain. Churches continue to fight a battle for the younger generation's loyalty. Some appear to be winning; others still struggle.

One type of church that is winning the hearts, pocketbooks, and commitment of Boomers and Busters is called the seeker-model church. Technically there are two types of seeker churches: seeker-centered and seeker-sensitive. This chapter will highlight the seeker-centered model and chapter 7 will focus on the seeker-sensitive model. Seeker-centered churches are also called seeker-targeted and seeker-driven.

By definition seeker-centered churches are those that target their Sunday ministries almost exclusively to the unchurched. The first and most publicized of these churches began in 1975 when Bill Hybels, who had seen his Son City youth program grow from twenty-five to over one thousand during a three-year period, decided to open a church that would excite nonbelievers. Along with some friends, he planted the nondenominational Willow Creek Community Church in South Barrington, Illinois. It is a uniquely successful church, averaging over fourteen thousand people in attendance each Sunday, with approximately twenty-five thousand at Easter. Hybels's message is centered on rock-solid biblical principles, and he preaches the same doctrines espoused by other evangelical churches. "It's just a traditional church that has put a coat of fresh paint on an old message," writes Tom Valeo, a staff writer for the *Daily Herald*.[1] Only the packaging is unorthodox—seeker-centered.

Characteristics of Seeker-Centered Churches

What makes a seeker-centered church innovative is its focus on the nonbeliever. Everything from the facility to the music to the message is designed to make a favorable impression on the unchurched person. It's a complete reversal of a traditional church, which tends to target its facilities, music, and message to the churched person.

In traditional churches everything is designed to make an impression on the believer, and evangelism most often takes a backseat to the discipling of the saints. In contrast the seeker-centered church places the greatest emphasis on evangelism. This clearly is an oversimplification of a complex approach to ministry but it is the essence of the seeker-centered approach. Seeker-centered churches usually have a mission statement that asserts: The mission of our church is to make fully devoted followers of Jesus Christ out of irreligious people. Discipleship is a vital part of such a mission but the stress is more on irreligious people than on the saints. Or as one person chose to put it, "The focus is on the undecided rather than the decided."

Seeker-centered church leaders see Matthew the tax collector as an example of their biblical basis for designing such a model of church ministry (see Luke 5:27–39). Once Matthew received Jesus Christ as his Savior, he naturally wanted his business associates to meet Christ. He instinctively knew, however, that he couldn't take them to the temple. It would have to take an unconventional approach to reach his network. The logical thing to do was to find a safe place where they could gather to meet Christ. Matthew hosted a party at his home with Jesus as the guest of honor. In this way his friends and coworkers could socialize with Jesus and his disciples in a nonreligious environment. Using this model, seeker-centered churches offer an unconventional service on Sunday morning, since that is when even the unchurched are open to attending church. The service is not a worship service but an evangelism service with a gospel presentation using creative and contemporary means. The seeker-centered Sunday morning service is entirely designed to reach the unchurched by delivering an uncompromising gospel presentation with grace and integrity. In the pure seeker-centered church, there is very little worship going on on Sunday mornings for a reason—it's hard to expect nonbelievers to worship a God whom they do not know.

To accomplish the task of reaching irreligious people, seeker-centered churches organize a remarkably sophisticated and well-planned ministry. While you may find some of the following characteristics in traditional churches, you will usually find most of them in churches that are seeker-centered.

Concern for demographic research. Seeker-centered churches take seriously the feelings and attitudes of the unchurched people in their ministry area. To find out what the nonbeliever thinks of church, research is conducted through a variety of means. The most common method of discovering the attitudes of the unchurched is to ask them what they think. This is accomplished in many cases through canvassing of neighborhoods to conduct surveys. Two simple questions form the core of the survey: Do you actively attend a local church? and Would you tell us why you don't attend?

Often two additional questions are asked: If you did go to church, what would you look for? and If a church were started in your area that was like what you wanted, would you be interested in receiving information about it? Seeker-centered churches have also asked similar questions by phone.

Increasingly, seeker-centered churches purchase sophisticated computer-generated demographics in an effort to gain further insight into the unchurched people in their communities.

The result of many years of asking these questions has been the formulation of some basic answers. Unchurched people say they don't attend church because it is boring, it is predictable, it is not relevant, and churches beg for money.

Profile unchurched people. Out of the demographic research a composite profile of the unchurched person emerges. The profile usually is given a fictitious name. In the case of Willow Creek the profile is of unchurched Harry and Mary. A California church profiles community Cathy and Carl (see below). The power of a profile is in giving the unchurched individuals in the community personality. It's easier to plan to reach community Cathy and Carl than some unknown entity called the unchurched.

Eleven Characteristics of Community Cathy and Carl

1. High level of education
2. Desire job satisfaction
3. Love the South Bay
4. Committed to fitness
5. Prefer a large group to a small one
6. Skeptical of organized religion
7. Enjoy contemporary music
8. Afraid of tomorrow
9. Both have to work
10. Prefer the casual to the formal
11. Overextended in time and money

Neutral church name. Willow Creek Community Church is a good example of this trend to select a generic church name devoid of any denominational connection. Unchurched people often don't understand religious-sounding church names that include words like *faith* or *grace*. Some individuals who once attended church remember it as a place with long lists of don'ts. Seeker-centered churches don't want the name of the church to trigger negative feelings. They look at their church name through the eyes of the unchurched, often using the following guidelines for selecting the name:

- a name that sets their church apart
- a name that attracts the unchurched
- a name that is simple to remember
- a name that helps people find their facility
- a name that removes barriers to attendance
- a name that communicates to the unchurched
- a name that expands their ministry area[2]

Nontraditional atmosphere. Seeker-centered churches deliberately avoid the trappings of traditional services by eliminating choirs, religious symbols, banners, pews, altars, holy inscriptions, and stained-glass windows. Gazing around seeker-centered churches one will not see a single cross inside or outside the church building. In place of the traditional church atmosphere is a carefully planned service choreographed like a professional stage show. The emotions of the unchurched are touched through upbeat, contemporary music, professional singing, and clever skits.

Practical messages. Messages are delivered in plain, everyday language based on everyday life. Emphasis is placed on communicating the message of Christ honestly and powerfully by any means and applying Bible passages to the typical problems that unchurched people face. Messages titled "Fanning the Flames of Marriage," "Facing Up to Our Fears," or "Home Improvement" are common. Messages must have what is called high "take home value"; they must answer the nonbeliever's question "So what?" The passion of seeker-centered churches is to communicate the message of Christ to those who are least likely to listen.

The essence of these characteristics is a high regard for the unchurched and their feelings. While not compromising the unchanging truth of the Bible, everything possible is done to keep nonbelievers from being turned off by the church services. Bill Hybels articulates the feelings of pastors who lead seeker-centered churches: "Our seekers want to be left alone. They don't want to say anything, sing anything, sign anything, or give anything. They want to seek from the shadows, and if we allow that, they'll hang around and sooner or later they're going to be moved."[3] Thus unchurched seekers are told to ignore the offerings and are not bothered by visits to their home, late night follow-up phone calls, or even mailers.

Believers are not neglected but offered an alternate worship service featuring lots of singing, prayer, and in-depth Bible teaching on a weekday evening rather than Sunday morning. Ongoing discipleship is encouraged through communities of small groups where members can experience personal growth and accountability. A high value is also placed on involvement in ministry, which is encouraged through personal recruiting of individuals to serve through activities and service to others.

Strengths of Seeker-Centered Churches

Without question seeker-centered churches contribute positively to the cause of Christ. The following is a partial list of their many strengths.

They fulfill the Great Commission. No one questions the fact that seeker-centered churches are effective in attracting the unchurched. These new models of church ministry do help the truly irreligious find answers to their complex questions. Many who would not step foot into a traditional church setting attend, listen, and decide to give their lives to Christ in seeker-centered churches.

They heal hurts and meet the needs of people. The stress on here-and-now problems naturally leads a seeker-centered church to develop ministries that are relevant to the unchurched. Ministries are offered that heal hurts and meet needs through support groups for single pregnant women, victims of incest, and individuals recovering from divorce; food pantries; activities for those in nursing homes; and assistance for those who are unemployed.

They bring new blood into the church. A key strength of innovative ministries throughout the history of Christianity has been their ability to bring new people into the church. Many seeker-centered churches promote women into positions of power and leadership, while many traditional churches still struggle with the idea of having women in leadership. Add to that the influx of new believers who are discipled, trained, and involved in ministry and one finds that seeker-centered churches are responsible for pouring new wine into the wineskin of the church.

They pioneer new approaches to ministry. Perhaps the most difficult thing to change in a traditional church is that which has been successful in the past. Existing churches tend to continue old ministries beyond their usefulness or sense of purpose. Seeker-centered churches ask, "What is the best way to meet this need?" rather than,

"What have we always done?" Energy is not directed toward maintaining the status quo but toward designing new ways to effectively reach the unchurched. This thrust leads to the creation of new approaches to ministry. One of the best examples of this is the use of short dramas or skits to illustrate the message. Using short five-minute skits to introduce the theme of the message is an approach that was developed by a seeker-centered church and has caught on even in more traditional churches.

They provide a new model of church. A great deal of interest has been given to new paradigms over the last five years. An obvious strength of the seeker-centered church has been its provision of an exciting new model of how church can be done, how the unchurched can be reached, and how discipleship can be effectively pursued.

Cautions to Be Considered

Like all models of church—traditional or nontraditional—caution must be exercised in appropriating the concepts and principles of seeker-centered churches.

Seeker-centered churches may be difficult for established churches to model. Church leaders who are serving in a church that was established on a more traditional model should be very cautious in adopting aspects of the seeker-centered model. As noted earlier, the essence of the seeker-centered model is a focus on the unchurched. This conflicts directly with the focus on the Christian of the more traditional church ministry. In almost all cases, it's next to impossible to transform a traditional church ministry into a seeker-centered one. However, there are some principles that may be employed to enable a traditional church to adapt itself to a seeker-sensitive model, which will be discussed in more detail in a following chapter.

Seeker-centered churches may result in a few leaders supporting an oversized ministry. Seeker-centered churches do attract nonbelievers. If the attraction and concomitant growth in attendance takes place rapidly, the smaller core of Christians may find they are the tip of an inverted pyramid—a small base of volunteers carrying the burden of too large a ministry. If such a burden continues on without relief, it's just a matter of time until the core volunteers become burned out and, for relief, try to return the church to a more traditional format. To successfully grow a seeker-centered church, it takes a sophisticated process to assimilate people into the life of the church, particularly into areas of ministry.

Seeker-centered churches may result in converts rather than disciples. For most seeker-centered churches, the mission is to make *fully devoted followers* of Jesus Christ out of irreligious people, which assumes a clear agenda for making disciples, not simply converts. Research among these churches reveals that a large majority have well-designed processes for involving people in small group communities, as well as for recruiting and training in ministry—both of which promote personal growth. In fact seeker-centered churches by and large accomplish these two aspects of growth better than traditional churches focused entirely on Christians. However, the seeker-centered church must be careful not to focus so much of its energy and resources on attracting and winning the irreligious that it neglects the ongoing discipleship of those it wins. Church leaders initiating a seeker-centered model are wise to carefully design systems for maintaining the spiritual growth of those who come to Christ in their church.

Seeker-centered churches may produce believers weak in biblical knowledge. One concern about seeker-centered churches comes from the preaching of what many call "light" sermons. Some have called the preaching in seeker-centered churches pop gospel, fast-food theology, and McChurch. The best seeker-centered churches are simply packaging the uncompromised gospel in a way that communicates to the unchurched. They are taking the timeless principles of Christ and presenting them in such a way that the unchurched can take them, accept them, and act on them. But admittedly there may be a tendency by some advocates of seeker-centered preaching to hype or dilute the message to attract an audience. True seeker-centered preaching is not dilution but communication of the gospel. Caution should be exercised so that the method does not overshadow the message.

Seeker-centered churches may result in a transient congregation. Seeker-centered churches have taken their share of potshots, most of which are distorted stereotypes that lead to wild conclusions. One common criticism suggests that while seeker-centered churches do win irreligious people to Christ, they lack effective discipleship or follow-up leading to spiritual growth. A fairly common comment heard around some seeker-centered churches is, "Unbelievers come here to get saved, stay two or three years, and then move on to another church where they can keep growing." If this is in fact true, then it will result in a transient pit stop type of congregation, where people stop to rest for a short time but eventually move on when the novelty wears off.

The seeker-centered model is one approach that is being effectively used today to reach unchurched Boomers and Busters. It is particularly effective when used in a new church-planting situation or in combination with the satellite and rebirthed models described in later chapters of this book. If the seeker-centered model interests your church, begin by reading the study of Calvary Church of Newport Mesa that follows. Then visit a seeker-centered church in your area and read *Rediscovering CHURCH: The Story and Vision of Willow Creek Community Church* (Grand Rapids: Zondervan, 1995) by Lynne and Bill Hybels.

6

A Look at a Seeker-Centered Church

Pastor Tim Celek

Tim Celek is the senior pastor of Calvary Church of Newport Mesa, 190 E. 23rd St., Costa Mesa, CA 92627, (714) 645-5050 FAX (714) 645-1106, E-mail: GenXfactor@aol.com

Walking through the corridors of the church where I was the singles' pastor, I found myself stride by stride with one of the members of the church's elder board. He was an incredible man of God. Approaching his late sixties at the time, he had a certain sense of winsomeness that seemed to draw many people to him. His faith was real, vital, compelling. I sensed a profound quality in him that I didn't have.

As we walked farther down the hallway, I thought I'd take a risk. You see, being twenty-four years old, I thought I had the world by the tail. Yet I saw in this man a uniqueness I wanted for myself. So I probed, "You're so alive. You're so engaging. What's so different about you?"

His response took me completely by surprise. He said, "I live out my life among lost men and women of this world, and I make it my everyday practice to live the kind of life that they'd want to aspire to someday." His direct answer was not what I thought I'd hear. But before I could ask him a follow-up question, he dropped a bomb of a question that I'll never forget. "Tim," he quizzed, "how many lost men and women do you know?" Stammering and stuttering, I answered, "None." I was appalled at my response to his question.

At the time I was attending one of the finest theological institutions in the United States. In fact I was enrolled in a class titled, "Evangelism and Missions." My textbook was written by one of the leading authorities on evangelism. I was ashamed to admit that I—a pastor on a church staff, someone who taught others about evangelism, someone who was enrolled in seminary, someone who was taking an evangelism course—didn't know even one lost person well enough to live out my life intentionally before him. Seeing my frustration, this wise older man encouraged, "Tim, I'm going to pray that God puts a passion in your heart for the lost. I'm going to pray that this passion gets translated into action."

In the weeks that followed, the fires began to burn. Back then I played racquetball frequently. Gradually I found myself developing significant relationships with many of the men in the league in which I played. It was great. However, during that time period something took place that was confusing to me. I'd invite these men to my church and they'd come, but many things at church didn't seem to make sense to these men. The songs, standing up as a first-time visitor, and the sermon were foreign to them. I felt like I should be interpreting the service to them as it unfolded. For the first time I was looking at my church, a well-known traditional church, through the eyes of an outside observer. Due to our relationship, my friends wouldn't get up and leave, but I'm sure they must have been asking themselves, "Why does a cool guy like you go to a place like this?"

It didn't take me long to figure out that my church was not the place to bring unchurched friends. But then, where could I take them? Eventually I began referring them to a local parachurch organization for businessmen. As the weeks passed, I began to think, *There is something wrong with this picture. This is the church. The same body of believers who found themselves "adding to their number daily." Why can't the church be a place for men and women like these?*

Three years later, with my church's blessing and support, I found myself planting a church, a church for people who didn't already go to a church and who didn't believe in God. From that encounter in the church hallway up to this point today, my life has been one faith-filled roller-coaster ride, one that I wouldn't trade for any other.

A Church for the Unchurched

Growing from a small core group of fewer than fifty people, today more than thirteen hundred men and women, boys and girls attend Calvary Church Newport Mesa in five weekend services. They come to hear the best news of all time—that Jesus and his kind of life is the greatest. More than 65 percent of those who regularly attend Calvary come from completely unchurched, nonbelieving backgrounds. Calvary is a church for the unconvinced. Calvary is a church where the music, the dress, the language, the topics, the quality shout loudly to the average nonchurched, nonbelieving person, "This is for me!" The term for this type of church—a church specifically focused on the "lost"—is seeker-centered. The weekend services use secular music, drama presentations, movie clips, video cuts of popular television programs, and practical messages all packaged in a fast-paced format to hold the attention of seekers.

Don't be fooled into thinking that our seeker-centered services are without substance. There is a solid philosophy behind this model. It takes more than using some surface methodologies to develop a successful seeker-centered church.

How to Go about This Yourself

Our approach to ministry shocks many people who do not understand the thinking behind the approach. If you're interested in this model, I highly recommend that you seriously think through the following foundational insights.

Be the Model

A popular saying suggests, "Image is everything." Unfortunately, most men and women in our culture misunderstand this to mean, "Everything is image." In a day and age of spin doctors, we've been conditioned not to believe and/or trust anything, particularly the church. It is imperative that the pastor or point person in a seeker-centered church embody and model a life lived out among the "lost."

People are looking for the real thing. There's simply no way a seeker-centered church can fly without the people at the point walking what they're talking. In essence, presence evangelism must precede proclamational evangelism.

Do Your Homework

Before starting Calvary Church, I surveyed people in more than two hundred homes and condominiums in our community. I stood in front of two local grocery stores talking with people as they went in and out. Since our church is located in Southern California, I even walked the beaches asking people if they'd answer two basic questions: "Are you a regular attendee of a church in this area?" If they said, "No," then I'd ask, "Why do you think it is that most people don't go to church?"

I recorded numerous responses. People told me, "Church is basically irrelevant to my life. It's just not real." Another was "Church is so stiff. Everyone seems so uptight. People are falling asleep. It's not alive." "Church people don't really care about others. They're so judgmental. They're in their own clique. I feel like I'm on the outside looking in."

It must be horrifying to God to see his truth and Son presented in the worst possible light. It's true that the greatest argument for Christianity is Christians and the Christian church. However, the greatest argument against Christianity is also Christians and the Christian church.

As I spoke with people I asked, "If you'd go to a church, what would you look for in a church that you'd attend?" It didn't take long to understand that what the unchurched seeker longs for in a church is vastly different from what a believer seeks. What I discovered from these varied responses eventually formed the strategy behind Calvary.

Please understand that the unchurched do not determine everything we do at Calvary. Our only rule of faith and practice is the Bible. But our desire has been, and continues to be, the creation of a church that removes *unnecessary* barriers to the unchurched. The reason? So that we can give them what they need—Jesus Christ. Realistically what's the alternative? A nonseeker-centered church? Do any of us honestly want to build a church that doesn't reach unchurched people?

Define Your Vision

The vision statement of Calvary says that we are a church that desires to *help people say yes to God in each and every aspect of their lives.* Burt Nanus says in his book, *Visionary Leadership,* "There's no more powerful engine driving an organization toward excellence and long-range success than an attractive, worthwhile, and achievable vision of the future, widely shared."[1]

I agree with Nanus. Vision drives all that we do. One thing for sure, if you ask almost anyone who serves or directs a ministry at Calvary what we're all about, they'll be able to tell you what our vision is and what it means. In a church setting, *vision by necessity must be* personal. Our desire is to communicate verbally and visually to people. People are our focus. "If anyone (personal) is in Christ, he/she is a new person."

Vision must be positive. We chose our mission statement mainly due to the fact that we're reaching a large number of Baby Busters. Generation X, as they are commonly referred to, has grown up with multiple negative messages. Junior high and high school campuses teach them to "Just Say No!" Since vision must be compelling, we make sure that people know that what we're all about is sharing the Good News of Jesus Christ. Our greatest desire is to literally help them say yes to God. We hope that Christ in us is so attractive that all other options pale in comparison.

Vision must be powerful. We're not trying to get them to say yes to Tim Celek or Calvary Church, but to God. Our desired outcome is that they'll see Jesus in us, and we'll become conduits to God the Father.

The vision that is personal, positive, and powerful draws people. One person put it this way: "Big thinking attracts big thinkers!" Don't forget the last two words of Nanus's description of vision. Vision must be "widely shared."

Building shared vision is probably the toughest job of the seeker-centered pastor because it's so elusive. Once you think your people get it, you suddenly hear one of your key leaders respond, "You know, I'm just not sure about this music we've been doing lately." Or "We seem to always be riding the crest; we're always out on the edge; can't we just coast? Don't you think you're being fanatical about always asking, 'How's this going to help more and more people say yes to God?'"

I've come to the conclusion that, due to the cares and concerns of this world and the competing messages, the nonpaid staff or workers within the church lose their vision for what it is they're doing within a twenty to twenty-five day time span. Paid staff begin to lose focus within two months' time. This is why I see as my primary task the communication of vision to the staff, the leaders, and the workers of Calvary. I'll do this many different ways. First, I live it. I eat, drink, and sleep the vision of this church. Second, we print it on everything from bulletins, to giving receipts, giving envelopes, stationery, fliers, and T-shirts. In other words, you can't miss it. Third, I'll communicate it through personal illustrations in messages or during announcements. Fourth, about every other weekend and in every one of the services, we'll have someone share their "story." This is the best way to communicate the vision. Someone who has said yes to God will get up and tell what that process was like for him or her. It is a real, living example of what we're about as a church.

During the 1992 elections, one of Bill Clinton's slogans in response to then President Bush was "It's the economy, stupid." I like to tell our staff when the ministry seems out of sorts, "It's the vision, stupid!" It may be too simplistic but much of what we're all about is communicating and relating a compelling, shared vision.

Know Your Core Values

Values are those elements in our church that we're willing to die for. At Calvary Church Newport Mesa, we strongly believe that

1. The Bible is the authoritative guide for life change.
   - The Bible is our primary grid or filter for all decision making.
   - The Bible is our benchmark for measuring right and wrong.
   - The Bible defines the principles necessary for right living.
2. Lost people matter to God, so they should matter to the church.
   - God loves all people no matter their state or condition.
   - Christians are to be the catalysts in outwardly demonstrating and verbally communicating God's love for the lost.
   - Our public events are primarily designed and/or targeted to be seeker-inclusive.

3. People who are truly committed to following Christ will progressively begin to think, feel, and act like Jesus would throughout their daily lives.
   - Maturity is not based on what you know or believe but on how you act and behave.
   - Someone whose life is truly changing will demonstrate the fruit of the Spirit.
4. The church and its people should demonstrate a deep and sincere love for God and others.
   - The practice of the people of CCNM and the programs of CCNM will at all times be driven by a commitment to fulfill the great commandment.
5. The church must be culturally relevant.
   - Our forms and methods of ministry will be understandable to our generation, as well as to the greater Southern California community.
6. High-quality services, programs, and facilities will positively influence people's perceptions concerning the church and God's work.
   - Consideration is given at all times to the aesthetics (the setting) of our facilities and programs.
   - In any given program, everyone has to do his or her best from start to finish in order to positively influence people's perceptions of the church.
   - A high-quality program includes thoughtful planning, excellent execution, and comprehensive evaluation.
7. People who use their gifts with a servant's heart in connection with others will make the greatest impact in the church and in the world.
   - Everybody is a "10" somewhere. Our desire is to help him or her find where.
   - Team ministry makes the greatest impact.
   - There is power in unity.
8. Small groups are the optimum place for transformational growth.
   - Small groups and/or ministry teams are a place to intentionally build relationships with other people and with God.
   - Transformational growth is a process where a person increasingly becomes more like Jesus Christ.
9. Teaching is most effective when the messenger is modeling the message.
   - People are more inclined to follow what you do than what you say.
   - We preach with our lives, not just our words.

Our ministry staff spends a large amount of time communicating the practical realities of our values to our volunteer leadership core through a monthly decentralized developmental process. Our goal is to have people in leadership who embrace the vision and values of Calvary.

Develop a Strategy

At Calvary our primary attraction strategy relies on our active attendees inviting their nonchurched friends to our weekend seeker services and/or life-stage events.

In the early years we did a number of direct mailers. I've found that quality, seeker-focused direct mail pieces do more to give a boost to our own core people than they do to attract large numbers of seekers. The best way to attract seekers is by word of mouth. When believers develop meaningful relationships with their unchurched friends and invite them to church, the seeker-centered model really thrives.

The Seeker Service

Everything that is done in our weekend services revolves around removing the barriers for seekers. We want them to walk out following the service and say, "I'd come back to this place." On the weekends we focus on a three-part grid. We ask ourselves: Is this real? Is this relevant? Is this rockin'?

Is it real? Oftentimes much of what happens in a church is syrupy, "pie-in-the-sky" type of stuff. A seeker's marriage might be traveling down the tunnel of chaos. His or her children may be unmanageable. Much of the time, the lives of seekers seem to be lived without hope. Then when they come to church, they find no answers. Indeed, many times seekers leave our traditional churches feeling worse than when they came in. Rather than helping them see that their burdens will be lighter if they follow Christ's directive—"Come to Me, all who are weary and heavy-laden, and I will give you rest" (Matt. 11:28)—some churches leave seekers with deeper feelings of despair.

On the weekends and at our other seeker-oriented events, we do whatever it takes to communicate the practicality of biblical truths. We use dramatic presentations to illustrate that we understand life as the seeker knows it. Many times we'll use movie clips or short takes from popular television programs to let the seeker know that we live in his or her world. (Of course, proper, paid rights must always be secured to use film clips.)

Is it relevant? One controversial hook that we seek to use almost exclusively at Calvary is secular music. For seekers, as well as for Christians, music elicits an emotional response. Most of us listen to music on our commutes to and from home. The proliferation of compact discs and cassette tapes is wide and varied.

Music, however, polarizes people. The type of music a church is willing to play indicates its willingness to venture into the world of the seeker. I see myself and our church as missional by our very nature. We are modern-day missionaries, seeking to contextualize the gospel of Jesus Christ in a foreign culture. We're trying to find secular hooks that can be redeemed for godly purposes. Music is a powerful hook. I can't begin to count the number of people who'll say, "I'll never be able to listen to that song the same way again, because every time I listen to it now, I'll be thinking about what you said." Music clearly shows seekers that we know their world and that we're not here to trash it, but we're leveraging it for supernatural purposes.

Is it rockin'? Everything is fast paced in our world. Some studies indicate that seven minutes is the attention span of the average adult. What we've done is to intentionally block our programing into six- to seven-minute segments. Our service moves. It's alive. We'll hear seekers say, "When I tried so and so's church, man I fell asleep, but not here. I never once looked at my watch. When it was all done, I left wanting more." Even in my messages, we'll put in video clips, short dramatic sketches, multimedia presentations, in an effort to keep people off balance. It's not predictable. It's planned spontaneity.

Developing Relationships

Our strategy moves along with intentional relationships with seekers, an invitation to a weekend or weekday seeker-focused event, and an invitation to join a small group. In the early chapters of the Book of Acts you see time and time again how real authentic biblical community was lived out among the lost. Lost people want real community. So our goal is to foster and promote multiple biblical communities in homes throughout our immediate area. Small groups become the vehicle where seekers can process the relevance of the biblical truths they're learning about, while at the same time watching others living and modeling authentic Christianity firsthand. We've carefully tracked new people since the beginning of our church and found that it takes a seeker approximately one and a half to two years to fully say yes to God. Allowing a person to process the claims of Christ is of high value. We don't see seekers as "in" or "out." They're just moving along the continuum to the cross. Small group cells are the foundation of the seeker church.

We attempt to assimilate people so they steward their time, talent, and treasure for kingdom work. Often this road is a long and arduous one. These three commodities are very precious and they're usually the last components of one's life to be relinquished to God's guidance and direction.

Finally, the hope is that the person who started out as a full-fledged seeker, and entered into a personal relationship with Jesus Christ, will invite others to experience the love and the joy and the peace that come only from God.

Some Mistakes I Made

It's exhilarating. There's nothing like it. It's hard work. It's messy. The lines are fuzzy. There's more gray than black and white. Yet there's nothing quite like seeing an irreligious person become a fully devoted follower of Jesus Christ.

I've made some mistakes along the way. Here are some of them.

I didn't realize how resource intensive a seeker-centered ministry can be. I'm convinced that many churches begin with a well-intentioned seeker-centered ministry as their focus. Then somewhere early in its development, they abandon their goal. They go from complete assurance that more than half their audience are seekers to hoping that on any given weekend a seeker would still feel comfortable in their midst.

Let's face it, it's much easier to plan and implement a set of five to six familiar contemporary worship songs, than week after week to thematically package, generate, and execute three "new" songs, a drama, and a media presentation. It's hard work to contextualize the gospel of Jesus Christ for a seeker audience.

In addition reaching seekers is not a lucrative endeavor. The per capita giving of Christians isn't all that great, but can you imagine a church where seekers outnumber Christians? The balance sheet isn't always pretty, but I believe the eternal rewards will more than make up for our present state of affairs.

I tried to do too much too fast. As pastors we tend to overestimate what can be done in a year and underestimate what can be done in ten years. My focus is no longer on the immediate, but on the long haul. I plan on being at Calvary for a long time. Besides, God's timing isn't generally my timing. If you think God is calling you to start a seeker-centered model of ministry, plan on being at the church long enough to see it happen. As a rule of thumb, plan on spending your entire life there, unless God clearly moves you away.

I didn't understand change theory and change management. Becoming seeker-centered requires a change in paradigm. As Bill Hybels says, "We're trying to turn atheists into missionaries." The tough part is that the initial core of workers comes primarily from traditional churches. The vision of a seeker-centered church takes a long time to resonate in the hearts of good, God-honoring people. In the early years, my worst enemy was me. I didn't take into account that people need time to process something new. I couldn't figure out why they couldn't quickly embrace something that I'd been thinking about for a month or two. The early days of Calvary were difficult, due in part to many changes that came too quickly. People were hurt, and that's never good for the kingdom of God.

In the final analysis, I'm glad I had that Spirit-led encounter in the corridor of my former church. Today my heart beats fast at the thought of the church becoming more intentional, more focused, and more effective in bringing the Good News to people who need it. When I get the chance to speak to church leaders, I always say, "Just remember the church is just one generation away from extinction." The church is the only hope for the world. I trust you'll want to position yourself and your church so that it penetrates a culture that desperately needs the love of Jesus Christ.

The Seeker-Sensitive Model

One new model of church ministry that has raised its critics' eyebrows and encouraged its supporters' smiles is the seeker-sensitive model. A close cousin to the seeker-centered model, it first caught the attention of church leaders in the early 1980s. While seeker-centered churches are primarily new church plants that target the unchurched, seeker-sensitive churches include congregations that use a worship style that is sensitive to the unchurched but does not exclusively target them. Seeker-sensitive churches may be defined as churches that target their ministries primarily to Christians while maintaining a sensitivity to unchurched guests.

A prime example of a seeker-sensitive church is Saddleback Valley Community Church planted by Pastor Rick Warren in 1980. Located in California's Orange County, it has created a wave of interest unmatched since Robert Schuller established his drive-in church during the 1950s and turned it into the Crystal Cathedral in Garden Grove during the early 1980s. Beginning with only two people, Saddleback has grown to over ten thousand people in sixteen years! It is the fastest-growing Baptist church in American history.

Characteristics of Seeker-Sensitive Churches

A creative profile of churches appeared in 1989, listing ten principles that are characteristics of seeker-sensitive churches.

　1. *Clear purpose:* Seeker-sensitive churches have a high degree of identity, a clearly defined target audience, and an evangelistic agenda set by the unchurched.

2. *Attractive worship:* Seeker-sensitive churches provide a casual, informal worship service offering excellent teaching and contemporary music.
3. *Positive leadership:* Seeker-sensitive churches have staff members who lead with vision and example.
4. *Inspirational preaching:* Seeker-sensitive churches offer preaching that applies the unchangeable Word of God to the everyday needs of people.
5. *Seeker focused:* Seeker-sensitive churches design their ministry with seekers in mind.
6. *Simple structure:* Seeker-sensitive churches are creative and flexible in developing new ministries.
7. *Culturally relevant:* Seeker-sensitive churches offer choices in programs and ministries.
8. *Meaningful relationships:* Seeker-sensitive churches affirm the natural networks of people through small groups.
9. *Innovative approaches:* Seeker-sensitive churches are oriented toward the present and future, allowing for creation of new approaches to ministry.
10. *Personal involvement:* Seeker-sensitive churches assist people to discover, develop, and use their gifts in satisfying ministry to others.[1]

Worship as Evangelism

In the seeker-sensitive church the service is truly a worship service where Christians feel comfortable worshiping while also bringing their friends and associates. There tends to be more participation from the audience through singing, clapping, hugging, and greeting than normally found in the typical seeker-centered church. Seeker-sensitive churches follow the example of Acts, where believers and unbelievers gathered together. As Peter preached, nonbelievers were powerfully convicted by the entire atmosphere, which included the clear presence of the Holy Spirit along with understandable teaching of God's Word.

"Seeker" is the nomenclature given to an unbeliever who visits a church worship service. Everything that takes place during these services keeps in mind that unbelievers are present. Because they may not understand traditional liturgies, hymns, or sermons, an intentional effort is made to be "seeker-friendly" or "seeker-sensitive." Hymnals may not be used. Sermons may be couched in easy-to-understand, practical living principles. Anonymity is always provided. Every possible effort is made not only to hold the seeker's attention, but also to avoid offending him or her at all costs.[2]

Newcomers Accepted

Seeker-sensitive churches take their lead from passages such as Leviticus 19:33–34 where God gives instructions to the people of Israel concerning the welcoming of outsiders into their midst:

> When a stranger resides with you in your land, you shall not do him wrong. The stranger who resides with you shall be to you as the native among you, and you shall love him as yourself; for you were aliens in the land of Egypt: I am the LORD your God.

Four principles from these verses guide seeker-sensitive churches. *First, respect guests at all times.* Seeker-sensitive churches give unchurched guests the anonymity they desire. They respect the privacy of seekers, giving them time to hear the Word of God and respond as the Holy Spirit moves them individually.

Second, treat a guest as one of your own. Guests visiting a seeker-sensitive church receive warm acceptance. Great care is taken to create a welcoming environment for seekers so that they can understand, participate, and learn from the worship service.

Third, love seekers as you love yourselves. Seeker-sensitive churches understand that acceptance does not mean approval. Believers love each other even though they don't always like or approve of everything that's done. Seeker-sensitive churches focus on loving the unchurched and giving God room and time to bring about the changes he desires in the lives of the unchurched.

Fourth, remember that you too were once aliens and strangers in the house of God. Seeker-sensitive churches follow Christ's words, "Let he who is without sin cast the first stone," by approaching the unchurched with a measure of humility that demonstrates that they know they are not perfect, just forgiven.

To create such a welcoming atmosphere requires a great deal of planning to "guesterize" the church.[3] Guesterizing a church means making a church more responsive to its guests and better able to attract new ones. In short it requires a seeker-sensitive church to

- give guests the best attitude: accepting and open
- give guests the best communication: clear and understandable
- give guests the best welcome: friendly and dignified
- give guests the best parking: reserved close to the entrance
- give guests the best seating: aisles and rear
- give guests the best time: before and following the service
- give guests the best service: directions and information

Strengths of Seeker-Sensitive Churches

As one might assume, the strengths of seeker-sensitive churches are much the same as for the seeker-centered churches noted previously. However, there are a few strengths that are somewhat different.

Seeker-sensitive churches are easier to model. The seeker-sensitive approach is easier to transfer to existing churches than the seeker-centered approach. It's nearly impossible to turn an existing church into a seeker-centered one. To do so takes more than simply establishing a new style of service. It takes a total recommitment of the entire church to a new priority to reach the unchurched. Seeker-centered churches also go by the name seeker-driven because their philosophy of ministry is driven by the desire to reach the unchurched. Established churches most often place an emphasis on believers. Reversing the emphasis from believers to nonbelievers, which becoming a seeker-centered church requires, creates a great deal of conflict.

It's much easier to make small adjustments to a church to make it more sensitive to seekers. This does not create major disruption. Thus the seeker-sensitive model is more transferable because it requires fewer changes to a church's existing services.

Seeker-sensitive churches give unchurched participants time to make a decision. Many traditional churches practice an evangelistic strategy designed to confront the unchurched with their need for Christ and to force an immediate decision. Deliberate confrontation takes place through a direct presentation of the gospel and a call for a public decision. Using an opposite approach, the seeker-sensitive church cultivates a church atmosphere that offers comfort to the seeker rather than confrontation. Since a confrontive approach may alienate the seeker, who may never return to church again, effort is expended to avoid a forced decision. The traditional church may use a "grab 'em and stab 'em" approach to evangelism, but the seeker-sensitive church uses a "hug 'em and love 'em" approach.

Seeker-sensitive churches restore balance for the Great Commission. It's no secret that many older churches are so trapped in their traditional programs that they have become unbalanced. The longer a church is in existence, the more stress is placed on educating the saints versus reaching the lost. "The seeker-church movement, perhaps more than any other recent factor, has caused us to ask ourselves and God if we are doing all that we can to reach the lost for Christ," writes Dr. Thom S. Rainer, Dean of the Billy Graham School of Missions, Evangelism, and Church Growth in Louisville, Kentucky. "The most significant contribution of the nontraditional church to the traditional church," he adds, "is the former's insistence that we must win a hearing from the lost and unchurched in our communities."[4]

Seeker-sensitive churches help the church understand its culture. Throughout its history, America has been a nation of multiple cultures. Even today travelers driving across the United States criss-cross communities called Little Italy, Little Poland, Little Germany, China Town, Little Saigon, and Korea Town. Yet for most of our history, churches have grown through biological growth—reaching their own children within their own culture. In the 1950s as children began to go off to college never to return home, churches capitalized on the transfer growth of "our kind of people" moving from city to city and region to region.

The American church is just now beginning to take seriously the multiple cultures and people groups existing in communities throughout the United States. In large part, credit for this goes to the seeker-sensitive church movement, which brought to light the need to exegete the culture as well as the Scripture. Discussing a strength of the seeker-sensitive church movement, Thom Rainer writes, ". . . the movement has caused many churches in our nation to have a heightened awareness of the culture and society in which they minister. Theology does not exist in a vacuum. It exists among sin-sick cultures that need to hear—in their language—the whole gospel message."[5] He further suggests, "The traditional church owes a debt of gratitude to nontraditional churches. The seeker-church movement may have its weaknesses, but it has taught us that we must be well-informed and sensitive to the cultures in which we live."[6]

Seeker-sensitive churches fill niches the traditional church ignores. As our culture has changed along with the unchurched, the traditional churched have circled their wagons and fought off the unchurched. They have ignored the unchurched because they are different and no longer willing to visit churches that bore them to tears. Lyle E. Schaller, a well-known church consultant, points out that ". . . the churches that are losing people in substantial numbers are not losing them because they have a very demanding presentation of the Scripture or because they're biblically orthodox. They're losing people because they're dull, boring, and irrelevant."[7]

One niche that traditional churches have largely failed to reach is the Buster generation. They have struggled to understand this newest generation and how to minister to it. Even though it is a generation looking for spiritual guidance, until the seeker church came along, few traditional churches effectively reached Busters. Opened in 1986, New Song Church in Southern California targets this young niche of the unchurched population. Since its beginning New Song has mushroomed to three services, drawing more than one thousand participants.

Cautions to Be Considered

Seeker-sensitive churches may lose focus. Leading a seeker-sensitive church is a balancing act. Church leaders must keep one eye focused on the seekers and one on the believers. The worship service contains a careful balance of ingredients that is at once meaningful to the saints and inoffensive to the seekers. It's easy to fall out of balance and out of focus by leaning toward one group or the other. There is constant tension due to the pressure to communicate to two groups of people. Emphasis on the seeker may at times cause a church to forget to disciple beyond the basics of the Christian faith. Dr. Rainer suggests, "With the emphasis on seeker-sensitive worship services, designed primarily for the boomer generation, the value of Christian education, Sunday school, has been obscured."[8]

Seeker-sensitive churches may create "light" worship. Some seeker-sensitive churches try to provide both worship for the saints and evangelism for the seekers within the same service. In some cases this may lead to a "lighter" worship service, since worship must be modified to appeal to the seekers in the audience. Verse-by-verse preaching, spontaneous testimonies, and extended singing, often popular with believers, must be abandoned for the sake of the seekers. Like the seeker-centered churches, eventually most seeker-sensitive churches offer two different services. "You can't chase two rabbits," notes author Rick Warren.

Seeker-sensitive churches may rely too heavily on technique. Direct mail advertising is a popular method for attracting seekers. It's particularly effective in communicating to Boomers who respond to marketing techniques. Current research has discovered that advertising techniques are not as effective with Busters due to a feeling that marketing is "fake." Busters especially hate being viewed as a demographic target. While marketing may be used successfully to attract people to seeker-sensitive churches, churches must not grow to rely too strongly on such techniques. The growing backlash against marketing to consumers is beginning to be felt by churches, and more importantly, a church must never allow marketing to supplant trust in the Holy Spirit. "A consequence of the seeker-church movement has been the embracing of seeker-sensitive methodologies without a grasp of the whole counsel of God—*in some churches.*"[9]

Seeker-sensitive churches may become a swinging door. Some studies report that seeker-sensitive churches lose up to 50 percent of their worshipers every two years.[10] The constant push to attract new seekers to church may result in poor assimilation of those who come.

While this is an issue churches have struggled with for years, it's one inherent danger of seeker-sensitive churches due to their heavy stress on the initial phase of attraction. All seeker-sensitive churches need to organize sophisticated processes for folding new people into the life of the congregation.

Seeker-sensitive churches may be perceived as too professional. Raising the quality of worship services and other ministries is a necessity in today's quality-conscious environment. To adopt a popular slogan, "Quality Is Job One" for seeker-sensitive churches. But people must see honesty and authenticity in the worship service. If seekers and members perceive that the worship service drifts more toward slick performance than worship, they will not remain long. Keeping the service worship-centered more than performance-centered will be an ongoing challenge for seeker-sensitive churches.

All pastors and church leaders tend to believe in church growth until another church nearby begins to experience growth. Then the churches that are not seeing growth begin to criticize the one that is showing signs of life and vitality. The assumption seems to be, if our church is growing, it's good growth. If another church is growing, it must be compromising. In the best light, such thinking is merely ridiculous. In the worst light, such thinking is pure jealousy. Many unfair criticisms have been leveled against the seeker-sensitive church model.

The seeker-sensitive model is a slightly different approach that is being effectively used by churches that cannot, for one reason or another, use the seeker-centered approach. If the seeker-sensitive model is one that interests your church, begin by reading the study of Harvest Community Church that follows. Then visit a seeker-sensitive church in your area and read *The Purpose Driven Church* (Grand Rapids: Zondervan, 1995) by Rick Warren.

8

A Look
at a Seeker-Sensitive Church

Pastor David Page

David Page is the senior pastor of Sonrise Church, 4035 Grass Valley Highway, Suite A, Auburn, CA 95602, (916) 885-9400, FAX (916) 885-8844, E-mail: sonrise@oro.net. David recently left Harvest Community Church, described in this chapter, to plant the church in Auburn, California.

One winter morning during my quiet time with God, I felt him gently impress on my heart that it was time to plant a church. At that time I was pastoring a forty-year-old traditional Southern Baptist church in Southern California, enjoying a full-time income with benefits. When I told my wife the good news about God calling us to plant a church she suggested, "Honey, I don't think that's God!" I asked her to pray about it for one week, and three days later she came to the same conclusion—God desired us to plant a church.

Beginning with prayer and using demographic studies, we narrowed down the possible locations for the new church to three cities. We eventually selected Palmdale, California, which at that time was the fastest-growing city in the state of California. We moved there in 1988 and began a Bible study in our home in February of that year. To recruit a core group, we ran a radio commercial on a local Christian radio station, and eight people came to our first Bible study. Three months later we began the church on Easter Sunday.

In preparation for our first worship service, we held a rehearsal service on Palm Sunday with seventeen people. Fourteen were from our core group and three were first-time visitors, one of whom made a commitment to Christ at the rehearsal! Twenty-two thousand direct mail invitations to the opening service went to the community two weeks prior to Easter. Since our target group was unchurched Boomers, the piece targeted those who had given up on traditional church services. Harvest was going to be a seeker-sensitive church. My first sermon series dealt with felt needs such as "How to Overcome . . . Fear, Stress, Worry, and Loneliness." For our first public worship service, we met in a hotel banquet room with 154 people in attendance. Harvest Community Church was born. The next week 80 people came back, and they became our initial congregation. We were off and growing.

First Steps

One month later we had our first baptism in a member's swimming pool. The fourteen new Christians brought their unchurched friends and family members to the baptism, resulting in seventy people gathered around the pool. From the very beginning we formed small groups and trained small group leaders. The small groups became the heartbeat of our church.

One year later the church relocated to an elementary school nine miles away. We lost about thirty people in the move but gained more than fifty people in the next three months. By 1990 two services were needed to accommodate the growing congregation. In 1993 we moved to a new high school in Palmdale, which had a large performing arts theater. We consolidated the two worship services into one service of five hundred people. Growth continued to accelerate, so that in 1994 two services were needed once again. On Easter Sunday in 1995, seven years after we began the church, over two thousand people participated in four services.

Style of Service

The worship services at Harvest are designed to attract and be sensitive to the needs of the typical unchurched man or woman in the Antelope Valley. We use contemporary Christian music, drama, and testimonies along with practical Bible teaching to make church relevant to the Boomer generation and the unique needs of the Busters.

Through a random door-to-door survey in our community prior to starting the church, I discovered the number one reason people didn't attend church was because they felt sermons were boring and didn't relate to their daily life. Thus our goal is to make church a truly meaningful experience for people—a valuable and worthwhile use of their time. When I pastored my first church (the traditional one) I was embarrassed to invite an unchurched friend to our church, and I was the pastor! I always wanted to pastor a church where I could enthusiastically invite my unchurched friends to attend. At Harvest I realized that dream. We developed a church that was seeker sensitive.

The music is contemporary and upbeat, played by a live band and sung by a group of singers who lead worship. We allow the unchurched person to check out the claims of Christianity in a relaxed and safe environment. Seekers like to sit in the back of the auditorium and they seem pleasantly surprised when they hear the music for the first time. During the worship service they may see a drama or hear a special music number from one of our gifted soloists and then a message from the Bible, related to everyday life. I speak in everyday language, teaching the Bible in a conversational tone just as if I were in their living room at home. I often use humor to get a point across. My message is simple and straightforward, and we provide sermon notes to help people follow along.

When people arrive at our church, they find several reserved parking spaces next to our main building. These spaces are reserved for first-time guests, single mothers, and senior citizens. The greeters at the door give each person a smile, a bulletin, and a warm greeting. Directional guides are available to help them find certain classrooms. The regular attendees and members at Harvest are very friendly and go out of their way to meet and befriend new people. Once the seekers get inside the building we leave them alone. An information table is available where questions may be answered as needed. During the welcome time in the service (which is after the first song) I get up and tell them how pleased we are they have come to worship with us. I let them know that we are not going to publicly introduce them, so they can relax. We offer them a free tape of that Sunday's message, which we send them in the mail if they request it on the welcome card. It's our way of saying thanks for taking the time out of their busy schedule to come and spend an hour and fifteen minutes in church. The bulletin they receive has a simple order of the service printed on it along with the songs we will sing that day. An invitation is given and then those responding are encouraged to use the welcome card to mark privately any decisions they make. We follow up on decisions during the week. The giving is done in a very low-key way. Prior to the closing song I thank our guests for coming and say a special prayer of blessing for them. After the service is over, we offer private prayer with our "prayer encouragers" in the front of the auditorium, and I (along with some other staff members) greet the visitors out on the patio as they leave.

Creating a Seeker-Sensitive Service

When creating a seeker-sensitive service it's important to develop the right atmosphere in the service. The following are four aspects of the atmosphere in a successful seeker-sensitive worship service.

An Exciting Atmosphere

David said, "I was glad when they said to me, Let us go to the house of the LORD" (Ps. 122:1). He didn't say it was a drag to go into the house of the Lord but that he was glad. Make church a celebration. Celebrate the Lord Jesus Christ. Build the worship service around a single theme. Contemporary dramas, testimonies from people whose lives have been dramatically changed, video, music, and multimedia presentations enhance the message as they support a common theme.

A Safe Atmosphere

The average unchurched person is afraid to attend a church worship service. He is afraid he might be singled out or made to stand up and introduce himself. He is afraid that someone might ask him a personal question about the Bible that he cannot answer. He fears that the preacher will condemn him in his sermon. He fears the possibility of people not accepting him for who he is. He fears no one will even notice that he is there and at the same time he wants to be anonymous. He's afraid he may see some friends from work who know what he's really like. He fears leaving his children in the nursery with unfamiliar people.

Because of the fears listed above, and many others, it is important to create a safe environment in your worship service. Don't publicly introduce visitors. Do allow seekers to be anonymous in your service. Let them sit in the back and check out the claims of Christianity from a distance. Don't pressure them during the invitation to become a Christian. During the welcome time at the beginning of the service I say, "If you're a first-time guest today, we welcome you. We're glad you're here! Don't worry, we're not going to have you stand up and introduce yourself. This is a safe place to be. We want you to feel comfortable—so sit back, relax, and enjoy our service."

To help people feel secure, I suggest you have greeters at the door and directional guides available to show people where to go. Have an information table with someone behind it to answer any questions seekers may have. We offer multiple worship services. On "big days" (more on big days later in the chapter) we also have parking lot attendants to help people park. First-time guests park up front for easy access to our services. When we started Harvest, we advertised in our mailout that a nurse (an RN) was the director of our nursery. This seemed to give confidence to couples with small children.

A Caring Atmosphere

A caring atmosphere is accomplished when the congregation is accepting, friendly, and loving toward seekers.

Accepting

All people have a need to feel accepted and sense that they belong. Learn to accept people just like Jesus did. As I read the Gospels I am amazed at how comfortable Jesus was around sinners—even tax collectors and prostitutes. He accepted them just as they were and he accepts us just as we are—warts and all! Accepting people as they are, however, doesn't necessarily mean that you agree with their lifestyle. One of our mottoes at Harvest is "We don't expect someone to act like a Christian until he becomes a Christian." Once they become Christians we seek to hold them to a high biblical standard, but not until then.

Allow people to come to church just as they are. Don't make them feel that they have to dress up. We emphasize that God looks at your heart, not your outward appearance (1 Sam. 16:7). Some people come in shorts and T-shirts, others come in suits and ties. Both are fine. I dress casually yet nicely to relate to everyone. I rarely wear a tie.

Friendly

Visitors in a congregation will rate a church as good or bad based on the friendliness of the people in that church. I believe the pastor sets the example in this area. If you are friendly to people in your church and encourage others to be the same, you are most likely going to have a friendly church. After each service I greet people out on the patio. I try to remember their names and give hugs to people if they let me. When we first started Harvest we used to have a five-minute rule. As soon as the final song was sung, our regular attendees and members were to find people they didn't know and befriend them for the first five minutes after the service was over. After that they could go and talk to their friends who came each week.

Loving

What's the purpose in having church if we're not expressing love to people? We teach people to love God and love others. We reach out to people through private prayer at the end of the service. We share "31 ways our church would like to serve you," which is a list of our various ministries that is printed in our bulletin. We take periodic "love offerings" for the homeless in our community. We encourage people to join a Tender Loving Care (T.L.C.) small group when they are ready. We emphasize that loving relationships are more important than religion. We attempt to treat each person with dignity, respect, and love.

A Learning Atmosphere

Seek to create a fun, learning atmosphere. I use humor in my messages when it is appropriate. I regularly share my failures with the congregation to let them know we are all human. I emphasize learning the Word of God. We place a high priority on teaching the Bible in a practical and understandable way. Actually I find that even seekers are curious about learning the timeless principles found in God's Word and how they relate to their daily problems. I use modern-day illustrations and provide sermon notes so people can follow along easily and retain more of what they learn. I try to show my enthusiasm when I teach the greatest news in the world from the greatest book in the world. We emphasize that we are a life-development church. We have a Life Development Institute that offers different classes on knowing Christ, growing in Christ, serving Christ, and sharing Christ.

Using Big Events

The growth of Harvest Community Church can be charted in direct relationship to the special outreach days we've planned. We developed four main "big days" each year. The four big days are Easter (spring), Mother's Day (pre-summer), Friend's Day (fall), and Christmas Eve (winter). It has not been unusual for our church to have more than two hundred first-time visitors on any of these big days. Other seeker events include a contemporary Christian concert in the summer and a Halloween alternative party in the fall. "Big days" benefit a church as they

- build morale and enthusiasm
- increase your prospect list
- make your community aware of your church
- enlarge the vision of members
- focus people's prayers
- stretch people's faith
- give members an opportunity to bring their friends and relatives
- increase the pool of volunteer workers

Successful big days usually have

- excellent special music
- a special guest (the key: name recognition among non-Christians)
- heavy advertising (direct mail, newspaper, radio)
- a special children's program (puppets, clown)
- good follow-up (a personal letter thanking visitors for coming)

Never give up your pulpit on a big day. Preach even when a guest speaker is present so the unchurched participants can get to know you. After a big day it's a good idea to plan an all-church fellowship to help get to know a lot of the seekers. In the past our church has reserved parks for picnics and sports activities, conference centers, and roller-skating rinks for these fellowships. They are a great way to assimilate new people into the church. We usually plan them one month after our big day.

Lessons I've Learned

I'm amazed at the way God blessed the growth of Harvest Community Church. God has confirmed his faithfulness over and over. Here are a few of the lessons I've learned at this church.

You can equip saints and reach seekers in one worship service. Many will tell you this is impossible and that you must specialize your services. We have found that you can minister to both groups by simply teaching the Bible in a practical and relevant way. Often I will speak to both groups during my message. For example, "If you've been a Christian for many years ..." or "If you believe in God but have not made a commitment to Jesus Christ ..." At Harvest we have consistently reached both groups on Sunday mornings. On Wednesday evening we have a service for people to grow even deeper in the Lord, but it is geared primarily toward believers.

Get people involved in small groups as soon as possible. We have seen accelerated spiritual growth in some of our new Christians, and this is in large part due to their involvement in a small group. Small groups are a great way to assimilate seekers after they come to Christ. I know of no better way to care for people in the church and to make disciples than by using small groups. I've learned that small groups are the key to leadership training. As you train small-group leaders, they in turn apprentice others, who eventually birth a new group. We have a high accountability for our small-group leaders. The result is that many leaders are developed and many people receive a high level of care within the church.

Learn to assimilate on the run. When a church grows very quickly, the tendency of some is to try to slow it down and consolidate. I've learned you need to learn to assimilate on the run. By this I mean don't stop doing what is causing your church to grow. Keep it up *while* you work to assimilate new people. You have to do both at the same time. It's even better to plan ahead for growth, but sometimes God surprises you. When a church is growing with momentum, never allow it to slow down, or it may begin to slide downward.

Every member is called to ministry. As we reach seekers we are constantly attempting to equip them for ministry. We developed a threefold strategy: Reach, Teach, Send. Our goal is to reach seekers, teach them, and then send them into ministry. We encourage people to come up with unique ministries even if we've never done them before in our church. We also encourage people to dream big. We have one couple at Harvest who developed a food ministry to the homeless in our community called "Harvest Oasis." They provide food, clothing, nutrition counseling, and many other services. They recruited more than forty volunteers from our church who share a similar passion and they now feed more than five hundred people per month!

Provide ongoing leadership training for ministry leaders. We call our ongoing training HALT—Harvest Advance Leadership Training. We offer it every other month and require our leaders to go if they want to remain in leadership. We have learned the best leaders are learners. I found it is helpful to have other qualified people come in and speak at these meetings. People hear me preach every Sunday, so it's nice to hear a fresh voice. Last year we budgeted a couple of thousand dollars to have some top speakers come in to teach at our HALT meetings. We feel our volunteer leaders are worth it. It's a good investment.

Teach the Bible. There is a tendency in some seeker-sensitive churches to not really teach the whole truth of God's Word for fear of offending seekers. This is wrong. As ministers we must teach the Word of God (2 Tim. 4:2). Some don't want to challenge people out of a fear of losing them. As a result, some may have watered down the gospel. Jesus challenged people when he said, "If anyone wishes to come after Me, let him deny himself, and take up his cross, and follow Me" (Mark 8:34). Jesus wasn't always seeker-sensitive or seeker-friendly. He spoke the truth even if it offended seekers or made him appear insensitive at times. I've learned that I must teach the Word of God and challenge both saints and seekers. Seekers will respect you for telling them the truth. God will honor his Word.

I use a variety of styles but I almost always preach a series. At Easter time and at our Friend's Day I do a topical series like "God's Blueprint for Your Family" based on Ephesians 5. Later I may follow it up by going through the Book of Jonah verse by verse and calling the series, "The God of the Second Chance." Topical or expositional teaching is not the issue. The issue is whether or not what you are teaching is biblical. Keep it in context, and let the Bible say what it says, rather than what you want it to say!

Teach about giving. In the early days of our church, we never mentioned anything about money. I've learned that not talking about giving hurts your people and your church. You may experience great numerical growth but you won't be able to minister to the people, care for their needs, and hire more staff if you don't teach biblical giving. At some point you will hit a wall. We did. I had to repent before the Lord and our people for not teaching them the truth about giving and tithing. Since that time, we have seen God do miraculous things in people's lives, and our budget more than doubled in a two-year period. It's really not about dollars and cents but about faith. Now what I say is, "If you are not a Christ follower, please don't feel you have to participate in the offering. But if you are a Christ follower, God calls you to obey him in the area of giving. We want to honor God and give our tithe to him, not because we have to but because we love him, as an act of worship."

Worship the Lord. In a seeker-centered church you would not ask seekers to fill out a welcome card or give a check, you would not put them in a position where they might have to say anything (even "hi" to someone next to them), and you wouldn't sing many songs in your worship service. But with a seeker-sensitive church model, you worship God. I feel that when seekers see Christ followers really worshiping God, it moves them. I like to call it worship evangelism. Worship is a big part of our service. We sing for twenty to thirty minutes, and we also use drama, special music, a contemporary choir, testimonies, giving, videos, and the act of participating in the Lord's Supper as forms of worship.

The Great Commission is for all races. We must reach out to all different colors, cultures, and classes with the gospel of Jesus Christ. Many seeker-sensitive churches are just Anglo churches. They have little or no ethnicity at all. I understand the homogeneous process, especially when you begin the church, but we must get beyond that. At Harvest we have a wonderful mixture of many different ethnic groups. Our mixture would be consistent with the ethnic makeup in our community. How did we do it? We began by staffing our church with leaders from different ethnic backgrounds. Next, we used music in our worship that appeals to many different groups. The style of music a church uses is a major key to reaching different ethnic groups. We also do dramas that have different characters from various ethnic backgrounds. We constantly tell our people that God is color-blind and we should be also. In our bulletin it says, "We welcome people of all ages and racial backgrounds."

Learn to be flexible. I've learned to be flexible and to put a structure around what God is already doing in the world. If something works, keep it. If it doesn't work, get rid of it. There are no sacred cows in our church. We have tried lots of programs. Some have worked marvelously, and some have failed miserably. When Harvest was only one year old, we went to a second worship service. It worked great at first because we started the second service on Easter Sunday. However, within a few weeks that new service, which had started with more than one hundred people on Easter, had only forty people attending, while more than two hundred were attending our other service. After a few months we decided to drop the new service and combine the people into the larger service. We had gone to a second service prematurely but had no problem cutting it when it wasn't working. About a year later we were forced to go to a second service because of space, and it worked out great.

Seeker-sensitive churches are being used by God to reach Boomers and Busters with the good news of Christ. I highly recommend you try it if your passion is to reach people for Jesus' sake.

9

The Blended Model

Several years ago I was being shown around a large Presbyterian church in Southern California. As the associate minister of music led me through the eight hundred–seat sanctuary, he proudly pointed out the massive pipe organ and then, unwittingly, commented, "We can't seem to keep our younger people." That comment didn't surprise me. It's one I heard expressed by the pastor of a Christian church in downtown Wichita, Kansas. It was voiced by leaders of an older, suburban Baptist church in Portland, Oregon. Lutheran laymen in a new area of Houston, Texas, told me the same story.

My guess is that 85 percent of all Protestant churches in the United States either are or will experience a significant challenge over the next twenty years to reach, win, and incorporate Boomers and Busters into their churches. Simply stated, the challenge is related to the fact that a majority of Protestant churches have patterned their ministries after models that may be dated pre–World War II. Those church models effectively reached the people of their day, and in many places continue to minister well, but for a larger number of Boomers and Busters these models are just not attractive.

In an effort to reach the newer generations, while limiting stress on their present members, churches are increasingly choosing the blended model. Indeed, some local bodies are already providing models of blended ministry. For example, the leaders of one church were shaken to learn that younger people were not attracted to their services. Through a daring move of strategy and faith, the pastor and leaders decided to launch a Sunday evening coffeehouse-style of ministry to be held immediately following the traditional evening service. The regular evening service began at 7:00 P.M. in the church sanctuary and ended promptly at 8:00 P.M. The new, contemporary group began at 8:15 P.M. and ended about 11:00 P.M., meeting in the church basement. As the two separate congregations grew, the pastor began a planned approach to blend the two groups together. While preaching to the traditional crowd, the pastor would often use words from new, modern songs as illustrations in his sermon. Later, while preaching the same message to the younger group, he would use words from traditional hymns as illustrations. In this way each group gradually came to understand and appreciate the music and preferences of the other. Similar educational experiences were used with each group to address other areas of tension. Points of common ground were established to draw the entire congregation together in love. Slowly a blended worship service formed, where both older and younger members enjoyed a sampling of the type of worship they found attractive.

The strategy to combine the elements from traditional and contemporary styles into one worship service is what distinguishes the blended model. Thom Rainer agrees that "'blended' typically refers to the combination of elements from the traditional and contemporary styles. How different churches 'blend' the two styles depends on each church."[1] He rightly understands that, "The central thrust of the blended services is to retain the music of traditional hymnody while introducing new music and approaches. The context and history of the church usually determine the pace by which new elements are introduced and the balance between contemporary and traditional elements."[2]

The blended model is much more than combining hymns and praise songs, organs and guitars, or choirs and praise teams. It goes to the depth of a church's philosophy of ministry. Where most churches have one basic philosophy of ministry, blended churches attempt to combine two differing philosophies of ministry. Over time the combination may eventually become its own distinct philosophy.

Characteristics of Blended Churches

Blending two styles of worship into one service is a sound approach for a church to take as it begins to move away from a traditional model. The subsequent characteristics are obvious in blended churches.

Two styles of music used in one worship service. The most obvious characteristic of the blended model is the use of two very different styles of music in the same worship service. It's common in a blended worship service to find newer praise songs used in combination with decades- or centuries-old hymns of the faith. Accommodating the use of hymns to a visual generation means the projection of hymns on slides or overhead projectors. Usually the worshipers are directed to the page where the hymn is located in the hymnbook, so those who prefer to sing harmony may do so.

Traditional ministries and new ministries exist side by side. Walking into a blended worship service one may see a small band on the platform making use of drums, a synthesizer, and a bass guitar. The worship leader may lead the congregation through a program of praise songs that includes a choir anthem. At a predetermined time, the choir members rise from their seats in the sanctuary and walk to the platform to take their places. Once in position, the worship leader turns to direct the choir anthem, after which the choir members move back to their seats. On some Sundays there may be a skit or a dramatic reading from the pulpit. Sometimes the pastor and congregation will read the Bible out loud responsively. At other times individuals located in various parts of the auditorium will recite a passage of Scripture from a modern translation. The blended church uses both traditional and contemporary forms of ministry in combination in an effort to meet the worship preferences of a diverse membership.

Changing terminology. One significant aspect of blended churches is the interchanging of traditional church terminology with a variety of new terms.

- The worship folder may be called a bulletin and/or a program.
- Newcomers may be called visitors and/or guests.
- The meeting room may be called a sanctuary and/or an auditorium.
- The entrance may be called a narthex and/or a lobby.

Experimental atmosphere. Blended services occasionally have a cluttered appearance. The addition of projectors, various musical instruments, and transitions between worship elements may give an appearance of confusion. This is true especially in the initial, experimental stages of developing a blended service.

Strengths of Blended Churches

Putting a blended model in place is more complicated than it first appears. It is worth the effort, however, since it brings a number of strengths to the church.

Blended churches demonstrate the unity of the entire body of Christ. A negative aspect of some newer models of church ministry is the way generations are separated. When a worship service is designed to target a select group, other groups will inevitably be alienated. A well-done blended worship service, which attracts members of all generations, demonstrates a unity that is missing in much of our society.

Blended churches respond to the various needs of different people. In our complex world, people have many different needs and preferences. By using a blended worship style, a church honors and responds appropriately to the needs of different people. Both those who like an upbeat style of service and those who prefer a softer approach find their needs met during the service.

Blended churches honor the past while moving into the future. The Holy Spirit has obviously spoken through people of all ages, teaching and admonishing through songs and hymns. Christianity began nearly two thousand years ago, and to ignore the wisdom and insights of Christian saints of past years is unwise. On the other hand, to live in the past is also unwise, since the Holy Spirit's creative work continues even now, which is why we are admonished to "sing a new song unto the Lord." Blending the best of the old and the best of the new into one worship service allows a church to honor the past and move into the future with balance.

Blended churches meet the needs of the old and the young. Pastors are fond of saying the church ministers to people from the cradle to the grave. This is one of the differences between a church and the so-called parachurch, which ministers primarily to a narrow target group. As Moses was told in Exodus 3, God is the God of Abraham, Isaac, and Jacob, which is just another way to say he is God of all generations. Blended churches seek to minister to the old and the young by providing a little bit of the style each prefers.

Blended churches give people time to accept change. Perhaps the key strength of the blended model is that it allows members to change at a slower pace. Members of the blended church may in time end up with a more contemporary worship service, but by blending styles initially, this church model gives people an opportunity to adjust. In many situations people are willing to change. They just don't want to do it too quickly. Questions need to be answered, feelings need to be addressed, and attitudes need to be adjusted. Moving too quickly into a new style of worship service does not give adequate time for people to vent their frustrations, let alone accept the new styles. Blending can be a process that allows time for change to occur at a slower pace.

Cautions to Be Considered

Blending different styles of ministry into a common worship service is an excellent way for smaller churches to keep hold of Boomers and Busters. If you see this model as one you desire to investigate, consider the cautions that follow.

It may be temporary. There is debate, but some church leaders believe the blended model is a transitional form between what the church *is* and what it *will be.* Others feel it is a true style in and of itself. In my book *Three Generations: Riding the Waves of Change in Your Church,* I suggest that, ". . . blending is not the destination but the journey, and where worship services end up stylistically may not be known for many years."[3] Holding the opposite view, Thom Rainer believes that, ". . . the blended style is developing its own identity and proponents." Further he observes, "The blended service may have begun as a transitional style, but it has become the style of choice in many regions."[4]

In normal situations, whenever significant change occurs in an organization, moving from point A to point B, the process includes a transitional phase (see figure 2).

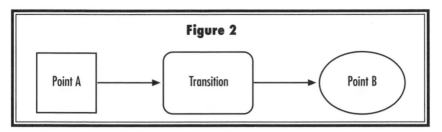

It is similar to heating an ice cube to the point that it becomes vapor. The ice cube goes through a transitional form, water, before it turns into water vapor. The water is a transitional phase.

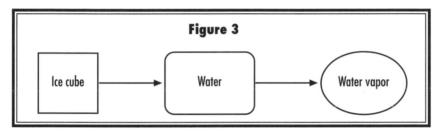

It's possible, perhaps even likely, that in some situations the ice cube will not be heated enough to become vapor and will remain in its transitional, water, phase. This may be what is happening in some churches that adopt the blended model as a transitional form and then find it works well enough that they remain in that phase. The transitional phase then becomes the permanent form of worship. A new style is born that will vary from church to church, depending on how the traditional and contemporary ingredients are blended.

It is wise to understand, though, that the form may be indeed temporary, lasting from five to ten years. When this is the case, the blended model serves to give people time to adjust to the forthcoming form without a lot of stress.

It may discourage leadership. The major criticism of the blended model is that it doesn't really meet the needs of anyone. When this unpleasant situation occurs, neither those who appreciate the traditional style nor those who desire the contemporary style are happy. Both criticize the blended approach, suggesting that more or fewer hymns be used, that music be played at a faster or slower pace, or that only the hymnbook or projection of songs be used. Neither group senses that it is receiving enough of what it desires in a worship service. This tends to discourage those who prefer using only one style of worship, since they predictably have strong feelings about the situation and aren't inclined to compromise for a blended service.

When only one style of service is used, the leaders gather at the core of the church, providing the vision for that particular style. The clear direction of the service draws those who can offer firm leadership to whatever single style is used.

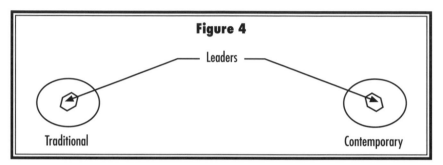

Figure 4

Leaders

Traditional   Contemporary

If the leaders become discouraged in the process of blending, they gravitate to the edges, criticizing the blended service and arguing for the exclusive use of the style they champion. If tensions escalate, it can lead to serious division.

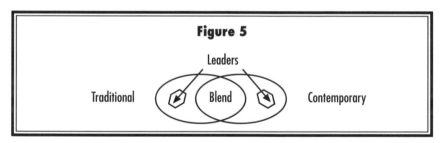

Figure 5

Leaders

Traditional   Blend   Contemporary

It may be difficult to lead and manage. A favorite movie of mine when I was younger was *Hercules.* I especially remember one episode when Hercules was captured and horses were strapped to each arm in an effort to rip him apart. With his super strength he was able to withstand the pressure from the horses and survive the ordeal. Those who lead blended services may at times feel like they have stampeding horses tied to their arms as they seek to hold the church together. The pressure created by leaders pulling the church in different directions can be difficult to endure (see figure 5). At times it will be nearly impossible to please the competing sides and to hold the church together.

It may result in serious disruption. If the frustration of the leaders increases to a breaking point, they may end up leaving the church and establishing a new ministry that focuses on the specific style of ministry they want. If the leaders of the contemporary side leave, they most often form a new church offering either a seeker-centered or seeker-sensitive approach. The blended service will then move more toward the traditional church service as the leadership drifts into the hands of those who are more traditional.

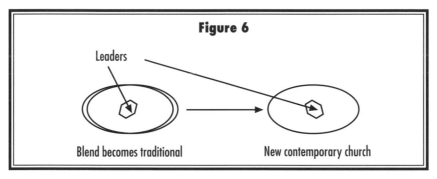

Figure 6

Leaders

Blend becomes traditional   New contemporary church

Experience has taught that if the opposite scenario takes place, with the traditional leaders leaving, some will end up attending a more traditional church in the community. However, others will go to a contemporary church that uses the same style of ministry they rejected in their own church.

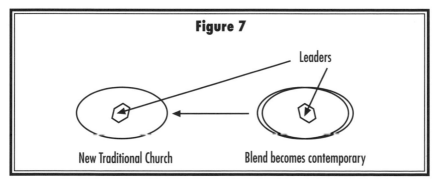

Figure 7

Leaders

New Traditional Church   Blend becomes contemporary

It may lose direction. If too many leaders end up leaving a church, then the church may find it is leaderless. When this happens, those who are left usually are less assertive in defining a direction for the church. In the best situation new leaders will emerge, and a new style of blended worship will come into its own, attracting those who prefer a little of the old and a little of the new. In the worst situation the church becomes a ship without a captain or a sail. With no clear direction, the church drifts along until new leadership comes on board to trim the sails for a new destination.

The blended model is one approach that is particularly useful for churches that want to honor the past while moving into the future. If the blended model interests your church, begin by reading the study of Grace Church that follows. Then visit a blended church in your area and read *Three Generations: Riding the Waves of Generational Change in Your Church* (Grand Rapids: Revell, 1995) by Gary L. McIntosh.

10

A Look at a Blended Church

Tim Ellis, Worship Arts Pastor

Dr. Mick Ukleja is the senior pastor of Grace Church, 5100 Cerritos Ave., Cypress, CA 90630, (714) 761-5100, FAX (714) 761-0200. Worship Arts Pastor Tim Ellis wrote this chapter with Executive Pastor Steve Schoger contributing.

After receiving two degrees in theology at Dallas Theological Seminary, thirty-two-year-old Mick Ukleja and his wife, Louise, accepted the invitation to become the pastor of a new church plant, Grace Community Church in Los Alamitos, California. A daughter church planted by Grace Brethren Church of Long Beach, it was three months old and was meeting at a local school campus with an attendance of about two hundred people. It was January 1981.

The Early Years

Right from the beginning Grace Church had a unique profile. The church was a member of the conservative and traditional Grace Brethren Church, a fellowship of churches not known for rapid growth. Yet it was full of dynamic energy, primarily due to the leadership of its young pastor. Shortly after arriving at Grace, Pastor Ukleja led the church to develop a mission statement, which has remained the same over the past sixteen years: "To glorify God by moving people toward maturity in Christ—helping them to grow in their relationship to God, other Christians, and the world." This mission has been the engine that has driven Grace Church through many changes and adjustments over the years, especially when it came to the worship service.

During the first seven years of ministry, Grace Community Church grew to an average attendance of approximately six hundred people and developed a strong presence in the community. The strength of the ministry centered around the relevant teaching and preaching of the senior pastor. The worship was primarily traditional, with a few praise choruses thrown in from time to time. Even though the church desired to move toward a style that would be more relevant to the community, the piano and organ continued to be the backbone of the worship service, with a choir and song leader in front of the congregation. Occasionally Grace Community Church ventured forth with newer approaches to worship on special occasions but it always returned to a primarily traditional model. During this same period, the church decided to leave the Grace Brethren denomination and become an independent congregation.

The Transitional Year

The new church was progressing well and growing when in 1988 an unusual turn of events took place. A Grace Brethren church in nearby Long Beach was feeling the plight of urbanization and decline. Grace Fellowshp Church, a large congregation of some one thousand Sunday worshipers, had experienced a very effective ministry over the years. Instead of waiting for the inevitable slow decline to take place, the church leaders considered their options. Early attempts to purchase land in another part of the city fell through, and the Grace Fellowship Church found itself going back to the drawing board. One of the options eventually considered was a merger with Grace Community Church. When the senior pastor at Grace Fellowhip Church accepted a call to another church, discussions about a potential merger accelerated. Later that year, Grace Fellowhip Church merged with Grace Community Church. The result led to four years of considerable excitement and chaos. To accommodate the sudden growth in worship attendance to nearly thirteen hundred people following the initial merger, the church was forced to use four different locations all at the same time. Shuttles were running, restaurants were converted into classrooms, movie theaters became makeshift auditoriums, and schools were redesigned. While all of this was essential to allow for the continued growth, it was a nightmare.

It was also during this period of time that an intentional decision was made to become more contemporary in worship style. The latter decision was very painful. The former members of Grace Fellowship Church were very traditional in heritage. In their former church, hymns were the norm and clapping was taboo. It seemed to many of the original worshipers from Grace Community Church that they were taking a step backward, while to some of the Grace Fellowship Church constituency, the church was leaping off the compromising modern deep end. As is normal when two churches merge, a gradual settling down took place, with some people moving on to other churches that fit their expectations more fully. As a rule of thumb, only about three-fourths of the total congregation of two merged churches remain one to two years after the merger. When the dust finally settled, there remained a church of some seven hundred weekend attendees, which was about 60 percent of the original thirteen hundred attendees immediately following the merger.

The Blended Years

In 1992, still driven by the mission of moving people toward maturity in Christ, Grace Community Church completed its wandering years and moved into a brand-new complex featuring a one thousand–seat auditorium, school and Christian education facilities, a nursery, and an office building. The new complex was located in the neighboring community of Cypress, and the word *Community* was dropped from our name, making us simply Grace Church.

One tremendous benefit of the merger was the addition of the minister of music from Grace Fellowship Church to the staff. Pastor Steve Schoger is a very talented musician and gifted leader. So, along with the merger, the quality of worship took an immediate upswing.

With the new facilities came many new visitors and a renewed commitment to the mission of the church. Over the years the defining values of Grace Church inherent in the mission statement have remained the same, while the resulting blended worship style slowly evolved to facilitate the mission with more focus and cohesion. In the new auditorium, for instance, there is no organ, the room is more like a concert hall or theater, and the seating is a combination of comfortable pews and chairs. A worship band has become a regular part of the worship service, and variety has become a key word in worship planning.

Believing that worship should be in the language of the people, we try to blend together musical styles that are meaningful and accessible for the churched and unchurched alike. Our services are thematic and planned to coordinate as part of teaching series that typically last four to eight weeks. Some series are topical, dealing with relevant issues head-on, while others are more exegetical, bringing out the relevance of the passage through verse-by-verse teaching. Whatever the case, all music is selected to complement the theme, direction, and flow of the service.

As a blended model of worship, we use hymns and traditional gospel songs along with praise and worship choruses. We do not blend the different styles of ministry out of obligation. Our approach arises out of our purpose. Often we find that an appropriate hymn is just what is needed to speak to an issue or lead the corporate body in a particular worship direction. At other times we choose a praise song or worship chorus. All music is selected with the theme and purpose of the worship service in mind. Some weekends there are no hymns and other weekends there may be as many as three. It all depends on the theme and the ministry team that is leading. We currently have three identical services: one on Saturday and two on Sunday. All services are called "Worship Celebration," which helps to highlight the blended style.

A typical service at Grace Church lasts one hour and fifteen minutes. Four to seven songs or musical pieces are used, including a time for corporate worship. Featured performance songs and, occasionally, instrumental pieces are other music ingredients often found in the worship service. In addition we use drama and video to add impact and variety to the service. Pulpit flowers, a regular aspect of traditional worship services, are often included on the platform.

Using Microsoft's Powerpoint presentation software, we project the words of songs for congregational singing from computer via two rear screen video projection systems, one on each side of the stage. This is a fantastic tool to blend praise songs, worship choruses, and hymns together as it blurs the lines that differentiate one type of music from another. Those who at one time may have preferred to sing only worship choruses don't always realize that they are singing a classic hymn. Similarly, people who never wanted to succumb to those repetitious choruses find themselves singing praise songs and enjoying them.

The lines of distinction between contemporary and traditional are also blended when it comes to our musical arrangements. Traditional hymns are often arranged in a contemporary style, and worship choruses may be accompanied by a chamber group. Content, substance, message, and effectiveness are emphasized over tradition and style. Quality is the overriding value.

Another distinctive feature of our blended approach is that although we often worship with a high-powered worship band, we also believe in the choir as the worship arts ministry community. The choir functions as a ministry team for those in our church who appreciate singing musical parts. With three identical services every weekend, the choir cannot be involved all the time but it averages a couple of weekends a month. The other weekends we utilize vocal worship teams. Most of the worship team members are drawn from the choir; however, there are some exceptions. We have five vocal worship teams as well as two youth worship teams that help keep the music fresh and varied.

We also believe in instrumental variety. Besides the worship band, we have an orchestra that plays four times a year, a big band, and a horn section that complements the worship band six times a year. We also feature a chamber group from time to time. Each performance group is also considered a personal ministry team or small group. The groups pray for and care for one another as they share the worship ministry together.

An integral part of our success in planning a blended worship service is what we call the "worship team." This is the brainstorming group that prays together and plans the direction of our weekend services. The team meets every week and consists of several pastoral staff, lay staff, worship arts personnel, and any additional staff who may be participating in an upcoming service. This group provides the creative juice for continuity with spontaneity from week to week. Teaching series are usually planned six months in advance. Knowing the direction of the preaching allows for general planning for each service to take place eight to twelve weeks ahead of time. Specific planning for each worship service is then worked out five to seven weeks ahead. A good drama must be rehearsed for several weeks prior to performance, and an original video piece can easily take a month to produce. To effectively implement the kinds of things we do, you must prepare and plan well in advance and involve as many people as possible, otherwise you'll burn yourself out, and that's not exactly what Jesus meant by laying down your life for your friends! Besides our worship team and our various music teams, we also have a drama team, a video production team, a video technical team, a video projection team, a sound team, a lighting team, and a soon-to-be-formed production team to work with stage management and coordination of the various teams during the services.

Before You Begin

Our best advice for those desiring to make the transition from an existing traditional worship service to a blended service is fourfold.

1. *Take it slow.* The ability to stay focused on our mission over the long haul has been a critical part of developing the blended worship style of Grace Church. You don't have to be in a hurry for long-term transformation to take place. We have the ability to respond quickly to cultural changes but we don't want to react hastily to passing fads or momentary trends. We believe in our mission and want to be intentional as we implement the vision that God has given us for Grace.

Be intentional but implement your changes over a two- to three-year period, if not longer.

2. *Use a team.* Put together a team of sharp people who have a heart for reaching the people in your community. Spend time educating them with available resources. We worked through Bill Easum's book *Sacred Cows Make Gourmet Burgers*[1] as a staff and with our elder board as well. The more people involved in your mission, the better. Pray diligently together for your community. Celebrate your progress and growth.

3. *Keep standards high.* Maintain a high standard of excellence. Excellence and sincerity cross over generational and denominational lines. If you're going to do it, do it wholeheartedly with lots of passion, and use the best resources available to you. Remember that oftentimes "less is more." It is better to do a little with excellence than a lot with mediocrity.

4. *Highlight your mission.* Speak your mission loudly and repeatedly, so that when changes are slowly implemented, people already know why and can share in the excitement of what God is doing. A key is to present your vision and mission in a manner that can be remembered by the congregation. Throughout the years more than eleven catchphrases have been used at Grace Church to communicate our mission. Note how they create a simple understanding of the mission, as well as communicate high standards.

Dignity with Informality

God's Word for Today's People

Values Driven

Principled Living

Don't Major on the Minors

Do What's Necessary Even If It's Drastic

Very Conservative Theology, Stark Raving Liberal Methodology

The Main Thing Is to Keep the Main Thing the Main Thing

Keep It Simple

Don't Beat the Sheep

Follow Your Good Intentions

115

A few rough spots were encountered as two congregations merged. Blending the best of traditional worship and the best of contemporary worship is a model that has helped us draw together members of all generations into one unified church. The resulting church is being used to reach new people for Christ as well as discipling the saints.

11

The Multiple-Track Model

Sixty-five-year-old Margie Thompson remembers being baptized in her church at the age of nine. She warmly recalls worshiping the Lord over the past fifty-six years with the assistance of John Newton, Fanny Crosby, Charles Wesley, and other well-known hymn writers of the faith. The quiet atmosphere of the worship service compels her to draw closer to God in silent preparation for the message. Familiar harmonies from the organ and piano bring back memories of close friendships, which only grow stronger over the years until interrupted as God calls some to go home to be with him. Margie's church, and its familiar surroundings, took on an even more precious memory after her husband, Bob, died three years ago. Participating in the worship service, she almost senses that Bob is sitting next to her in the pew as he did for so many years.

Thirty-nine-year-old Christy Simmons accepted Christ just a little over one year ago. She joined the church three months later, anticipating the new joy Christ and Christian friends would bring into her life. Unlike Margie, Christy grew up listening to Elton John, the Beatles, and the Rolling Stones, and she enjoys the local classic-rock radio station. Christy's husband, Mike, often leads worship with his electric guitar. It seems like they sing a "new song unto the Lord" almost every week. They both look forward to the short drama sketches that introduce the pastor's message.

Both Margie and Christy are faithful worshipers in their church. While they have different preferences for worship style, it hasn't stopped them from ministering to one another. Margie has encouraged Christy with insights on how to raise a strong-willed child, and Christy has invited Margie over for meals during holidays. Although they have diverse interests and styles, they are working together in the same body of Christ. Potentially incompatible in their desires for different styles of worship experience, how does it happen that they get along in the same church?

Margie and Christy worship and minister in the same church because it uses a multiple-track model of ministry. Multiple-track churches are those that offer distinct approaches to worship at different times. The name may sound familiar to those involved in educational circles where multiple tracks have been commonly used since the 1950s. For example, high schools often use a multiple-track approach with freshmen, beginning classes at 8:00 A.M., followed by sophomores at 9:00 A.M., and juniors and seniors at 10:00 A.M. An even more familiar example is the use of multiple tracks in year-round schools. Children are placed in different tracks and attend school at different times throughout the year.

Characteristics of Multiple-Track Churches

Traditional churches increasingly find that they attract the "Margies" but not the "Christys" of the world. Those churches that seek new church growth in an old church discover that secular people under the age of fifty often do not appreciate a traditional worship service. Since traditional worship services trace their roots back to before the 1950s, they reflect a culture that no longer exists. As a result, multiple-track churches determine to offer two or more different worship services to meet the needs of the "Margies" and "Christys." One of the trends being observed among growing churches today is the addition of multiple worship services. While adding a second service is not a new idea, some churches are now adding a third, a fourth, and even a fifth service on nights not normally used for worship in Protestant churches.

Different Styles of Worship

The prime characteristic of multiple-track churches is the offering of two or more styles of worship services. Each worship service targets a different group of people who have expressed a desire for distinct forms of worship. Churches continue to offer a traditional service to minister to the "Margies," who appreciate the old hymns of the faith. Then, during a different time slot, they add a contemporary service aimed at the "Christys" of the community, who are unfamiliar with church traditions. As an example, a multiple-track church might offer two contrasting services as follows.

Contemporary Service	Traditional Service
9:30–10:30 A.M.	11:00–12:00 noon
casual dress	dressed up
applause acceptable	applause not encouraged
guests anonymous	visitors greeted
low-key challenge	invitation at close of sermon
varied format	consistent format
shorter sermon	longer sermon
modern praise songs	old hymns of the faith
small band (guitars and drums)	piano and organ
pastor dressed down	pastor dressed up
male and female ushers	only male ushers
audio/visual support	rare audio/visual support
praise group (four to five singers)	choir
worship leader	song leader
regular use of drama	skits on special occasions
contemporary music	traditional church music
no baptism or communion	baptism and communion
few announcements	lots of announcements

Some churches may even take the multiple-track approach to the limit, giving people a choice of three or four services designed in contrasting styles. For example, a church may offer three or four worship services, each targeted to reach a specific group of people. One pastor describes his multiple-track worship services as traditional, loud, louder, and loudest! The schedule of service for such a church might look like the following.

Saturday Evening

    7:00–8:15 P.M.   Celebration worship service (up-tempo)

Sunday Morning

    8:15–9:15 A.M.   Praise service (softer contemporary)

    9:30–10:30 A.M.   Contemporary service (upbeat contemporary)

    11:00–12:00 noon   Traditional worship service

Music to Taste

Many people today legitimately prefer contemporary praise music to enhance their worship. Others legitimately prefer traditional hymns or anthems to enhance their worship. A multiple-track model of ministry flavors each worship service specifically to meet the different musical tastes of diverse people.

Sermons Meet Needs

As people progress through various life stages, it's natural for them to encounter needs that are quite different from those faced at other life stages. Emerging adults tend to be interested in establishing families, finding a job, buying a home, and developing their own identity. In contrast middle adults are more interested in developing grandparenting skills, downsizing their home, saving for retirement, and staying healthy. Preparing messages that speak to a multi-generational congregation has always had its difficulties, but in today's rapidly changing culture, it is even more difficult. Multiple tracks of worship in a local church allow the pastor to tailor the message to each congregation by selecting illustrations, stories, and wording that communicate clearly to each one.

Multiple-Track Approaches

There are three basic approaches to scheduling multiple worship services on Sunday mornings. Most churches find it best to move progressively from one approach to another as they experience growth.

120

The Sandwich Approach

For churches with a traditional schedule of Sunday school followed by morning worship, the easiest transition to a multiple track is to use the sandwich approach. The sandwich approach simply adds a second worship service before Sunday school, sandwiching Sunday school between two worship services. This approach is the easiest way to begin since it creates the least disruption to the schedule already in place.

The Flip-Flop Approach

Churches using the flip-flop approach offer two worship services and two Sunday schools together. Ministry personnel may then flip-flop back and forth between services, working in one and attending another. Likewise, this model gives people who attend the first worship service opportunity to cross over and attend the second Sunday school. Those who attend Sunday school during the first service may then cross over and attend the second worship service.

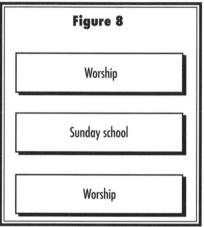

Figure 8

Worship

Sunday school

Worship

Figure 9

Worship	Sunday school
Worship	Sunday school

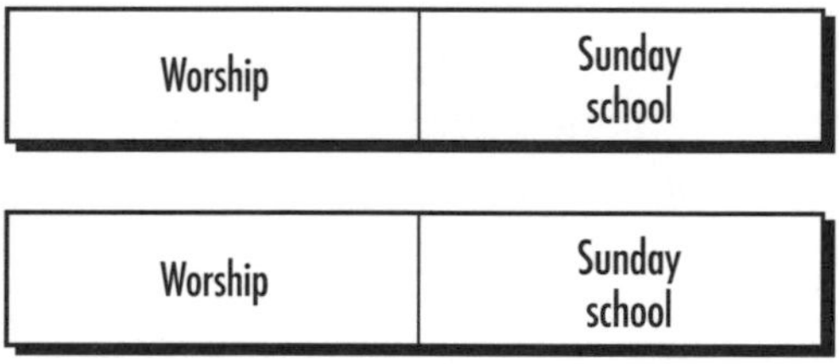

The Consecutive Approach

Churches that experience continual growth often hold three consecutive worship services on Sunday mornings. Most will offer only two complete Sunday schools with limited child care during one service.

Some churches find that Thursday, Friday, or Saturday evenings are good times for adding another worship track. Churches interested in pursuing an evening worship service should be aware that evening worship services are normally a spillover of an already strong Sunday morning ministry,

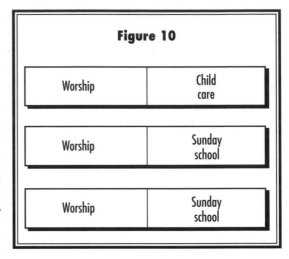

Figure 10

Worship	Child care
Worship	Sunday school
Worship	Sunday school

tend to have a more casual and laid-back atmosphere than on Sunday morning, often lack the same intensity of Sunday morning services as worshipers come directly from work or other activities and may be tired, and are a good option for people who work on weekends and/or prefer to use the weekend for travel or recreational activities.

Strengths of Multiple-Track Churches

The multiple-track approach to worship affirms the different interests, needs, and identities of all those attending a church. By offering options, a church has the opportunity to discover several strengths among its members that it might not have otherwise discovered.

Multiple-track churches broaden a church's outreach. Churches like to believe they minister to all kinds of people, but cultural limitations focus a church on a fairly narrow segment of the population. Multiple worship services broaden a church's outreach by affirming the Christian cultural tradition while advancing a new model(s) directed to the current tastes of a new culture. By offering more than one type of worship service, a church affirms the old while confirming the new. The church reaches a broader cultural mix, enlarging its outreach potential.

Multiple-track churches meet the needs of different people. Without doing away with any type of service, a multiple-track church adds a new one to provide optional ways to meet with God. The traditional service draws those who want to hear the small voice of God in a quiet reverent atmosphere. A contemporary service pulls in those who are looking to celebrate the resurrection of Jesus Christ in an upbeat way.

Multiple-track churches provide people a choice. Growing up in the United States provides people with an array of choices. Shopping at the local mall, one may find more than one hundred stores under the same roof along with several fast-food restaurants where shoppers may eat. People desire and expect options whether they are buying clothes or looking for a worship service. Multiple-track churches provide people with a choice of worship time and worship style. One style and time for worship gives a visitor two choices: stay or leave. There is a 50/50 chance that the visitor will not return. Two worship services give visitors three choices: attend the first service, attend the second service, or leave. Note that the third option—leaving—is reduced to 33 percent. If a church is fortunate enough to offer three worship services, visitors now have four choices: attend one of the services or leave. But now there is only a 25 percent chance they will leave, while the potential that they will find a service they like is increased to 75 percent! An increase in choice means that a church is more likely to meet the needs of visitors so that they stay and become a part of the church.

Multiple-track churches increase ministry opportunities. A natural by-product of multiple-track worship services is the creation of a variety of ministry opportunities. The person who enjoys singing harmony in a large choir finds ample opportunity to do so. At the same time, talented musicians who play guitars, drums, and electric keyboards find a place to serve as well. Those who appreciate dressing up for church find acceptance, as do those who dress more casually.

Multiple-track churches generate cross-generational awareness. At first glance one might assume that multiple-track churches cause a breakdown in communication between the generations. While this is a valid concern, multiple tracks are no different than life-stage divisions in other areas of church life such as in the Sunday school.

In general, multiple-track churches find that there is a good mix of different age groups in every service. Many younger people appreciate the great hymns of the faith and will attend the traditional service. As expected, some older members enjoy the upbeat excitement of the new forms of music and worship and attend the more contemporary service. This cross-pollination of people in different worship services encourages a better understanding of the generations.

Seven Reasons to Use a Multiple-Track Model

1. *Provide options.* Adding a new worship service is one way to provide choices in church ministry.
2. *Maximize space.* Multiple services allow a church to use its present space to greater advantage without having to engage in an expensive building program.
3. *Allow for growth.* An overcrowded auditorium actually discourages numerical growth.
4. *Increase faith.* Churches that offer more than one worship service tend to place an emphasis on reaching newer members, which takes vision and faith.
5. *Enlarge ministry.* By adding additional services, a church nearly doubles the ministry roles and tasks where people may become involved.
6. *Reach new people.* By adding an additional service with a differing time and style, a church can attract new people who might not normally attend.
7. *Keep people happy.* Multiple services allow for a church to zero in on varied preferences.

Cautions to Be Considered

No church can introduce a change in ministry style as dramatic as a multiple-track approach without undergoing significant backlash. Resistance and concern revolve around the following areas.

One service may be viewed as more spiritual. In the initial stages of development, some may perceive the traditional style of worship as more spiritual than the contemporary one. The idea suggests that once the younger people grow up, they will accept the traditional worship as the proper form. Those who prefer the contemporary approach to worship may look down on the traditional worship service as being cold and void of God's Spirit. It is vital that neither service be viewed as better or worse than the other. Care must be taken to communicate that both are necessary to provide a worship experience that is relevant to the people they are designed to reach.

One worship service may grow larger than another. The region in which the church is located, the musical tastes of those in the congregation, or the time of the services may lead to one service growing larger than the other. For example, in sunnier climates some may attend the earlier services in order to have a larger part of the day available for recreation. Thus the earlier service may grow larger due to convenience rather than preference for its style. In other areas of the country one service may become larger due to the style of worship offered. As a rule of thumb, just the addition of a second service will draw an additional 10 percent to 20 percent of new people due to the choice of a different time.

The service that starts between 9:00 A.M. and 10:00 A.M. will often be the largest. In the initial stages one service will have about two-thirds of the total attendance and the other one-third. The key is not to have an empty feeling in any worship service. A service with fewer than 35 percent of the seats filled is uncomfortable. The determination of a service as empty or full is based more on the seats available than the actual size of the room. If possible, remove chairs or pews and widen aisles to make the worship service seem fuller. The church should be directed to rejoice in the added blessing God brings through multiple worship tracks rather than allowed to focus on the growth of one service over another.

Ministry will increase in complexity. By adding additional worship service tracks, the complexity of the overall ministry increases. This complexity will be felt in the additional use of the facilities, the need for multiple worship personnel (musicians, ushers, and so on), and the added stress on those who must be at church during all worship tracks. The pastor confronts increased complexity in sermon preparation, as he must develop a message that is modified to each particular congregation. In essence the pastor and worship leader must carry around in their minds two or more slightly different philosophies of ministry. Ministry to one congregation must be accomplished in one way. Then, just a few minutes later, the ministry to another congregation must be done in a slightly different format.

Child care tends to be the biggest headache. Churches are finding it increasingly difficult to recruit volunteer or even paid child-care workers. With the addition of a second or third worship track, providing workers for this necessary ministry becomes an even larger obstacle to overcome.

Business meetings may be underattended by the younger generation. Churches that use a congregational style of decision making will occasionally discover that business meetings are stacked against the younger generation. This usually occurs when the majority of younger people attend the earlier worship service, and the older generation attends the later service. Business meetings will most often be scheduled following the last service or occasionally in the evening. When this takes place, younger people do not stay around or return for the business meeting, which leaves the Builders to make all the decisions. To overcome this tendency, churches find that business meetings must be held at other times, frequently in the evening as a social gathering to attract the younger group.

The goal of a church is simple. It's to introduce people to Jesus Christ in a clear way so that they can decide to follow him. The multiple-track model of ministry is one way churches are reaching out to aging Boomers and emerging Busters without ignoring the needs of the older Builders in their congregations. In the United States, Sunday morning is the time that people without Christ will visit a church to check out Christianity. By offering different styles of worship service, churches find that they are able to reach new people for Christ. An old church can thus renew itself through a multiple-track approach. If the multiple-track model interests your church, begin by reading the study of Community Baptist Church that follows. Then visit a multiple-track church in your area and read *Let It Grow!* (Grand Rapids: Baker, 1993) by Josh Hunt.

12

A Look at a Multiple-Track Church

Dr. Glen S. Martin

Dr. Glen S. Martin is the senior pastor of Community Baptist Church, 1243 Artesia Blvd., Manhattan Beach, CA 90266-6997, (310) 372-4641, FAX (310) 374-4789, E-mail: glen@cdcmb.org.

A church of fewer than five hundred members that would average two thousand in nine years—this was the vision I had for my new pastorate at Community Baptist Church when I accepted our Lord's call to a new pastorate in 1991.

Community Baptist Church was founded in 1911 and had from its very inception been seen as the "lighthouse in the South Bay." In 1957 the church relocated from a small facility in Hermosa Beach to its present location in Manhattan Beach, California.

Being a part of the Conservative Baptist Association, it had always placed a high priority on missions but had not invested a lot of finances or energy in reaching the South Bay community. In 1988 the leadership team of the church designated "Touching our community with the reality of Jesus Christ" as the new mission statement for Community Baptist. Two years later the pastor before me was called to a teaching position after making substantial headway in turning the church toward this vision. It was at this time that I was contacted to consider the pastorate.

Clarifying Worship Styles

When I arrived at CBC, I discovered a church with a long history of tradition, and those who wanted to add new types of ministry had faced strong opposition and hostility. The church had already started a second morning service, which they called their contemporary service. However, the church was still overcoming the problems created by the previous music director who was convinced that the contemporary minded needed to know and sing the "old hymns of the faith," and that the more traditional minded should be stretched to include some of the more modern choruses. The result? Both worship services ended up being blended. With this dual emphasis in both services, the people were confused and somewhat bitter.

During the candidating process the hot questions concerned my stance on blended services, what plan I had for the traditional services, and what changes I envisioned down the road for worship. There was both a feeling of expectation and fear permeating the church about what might happen after I became pastor. Throughout the "calling" process I verbalized my support of both the contemporary and the traditional worship services. My first task after accepting the church's call would be to settle the dispute between worship styles by clearly offering both preferences of worship in separate services. The early service was to be 100 percent contemporary and the later service 100 percent traditional.

Within the first six months of my pastorate, we established two distinct types of service. The 8:30 A.M. service became the contemporary service, with a live praise band, casual dress, and predominantly praise music. I preached without notes, moving around the platform with the aid of a wireless microphone. The pulpit was removed, and I dressed in nice casual slacks and shirt. The 11:00 A.M. service became the traditional service, using organ, piano, and a full-robed choir. Between the two services I changed into a suit to preach, and the pulpit was returned to its regular place. The two distinct services targeted a different audience. The message was the same in each of these services, with some adaptation of illustrations to apply the message specifically to each target congregation.

Numerous questions and emotional struggles occurred during the initial transition. "We don't know everyone in the church anymore," was a common complaint. This proved to be true. The two services were very different, with contrasting demeanor and expressions. "We don't get to see the young people." This too was true. But with the changing climate in many of the churches in our area toward a more contemporary ministry, we might not get to see these young people anyway, as they would soon be attending another fellowship not far away. "Are you just trying to pacify the traditional folks until we die off?" This fear was one only time would relieve. I wanted the people to understand that I was totally committed to reaching people of all ages through two styles of worship and would do whatever it took to accomplish this vision.

Moving Forward

The model we had chosen to follow, although we had not given it a name yet, was the multiple-track model, a term that has been popularized by Josh Hunt in his book *Let It Grow!* The multiple-track approach can be summarized as a congregation that sees itself as a church of interrelated congregations with several preaching pastors and numerous meeting times both for worship services and small groups. The church will not purchase facilities large enough for the entire congregation to meet in, although they may rent such facilities on an occasional basis.

There are two primary advantages of the multiple-track approach. The first is the tremendous savings on capital resources. This savings has the advantage of reducing the pressure on a congregation to raise the funds needed to build a large auditorium. It also frees money to be spent on local outreach, missions, advertising, and additional staff.

The second advantage of the multiple-track approach is the diversity of programing it enables the church to offer its people. Especially in the 90s, people are very different. By offering different approaches in worship services, we can be more effective in reaching a larger number of people.[1]

It was not long before the 8:30 A.M. service became comfortably full and plans were developed to start an additional service. We polled the congregation, trying to decipher if this would be the opportune time to begin a Saturday evening service rather than add another on Sunday morning. The response was overwhelming support of the Saturday night concept, but we would not be able to muster the critical mass, about 250 people, to have this service be the success we wanted. So a 9:30 A.M. service was started. Now I was preaching at 8:15, 9:30, and 11:00 every Sunday morning. The first two services were contemporary and the third traditional. Once again fear was expressed that eventually the traditional service would be canceled. Again I lovingly told the congregation, "I am just as committed to the traditional service as I am to the contemporary services. I want all three to continue to reach people for Christ."

By this time, after about a three-year tenure, I found my leadership gaining credibility. That does not mean that I had not encountered my fair share of opposition. There were several power struggles along the way, but I was convinced not only of God's hand in my call to this church but also God's ratification of our ministry as we saw more than one hundred people give their lives to Jesus in 1993. Our attendance had grown from 450 to 700 to 900 people during the initial changes and was soon breaking 1,000 regularly when the third service was added. Our desire was never to steal sheep from other fellowships, so we rarely advertised in the church page (which had been the predominant form of advertisement before my arrival). Now our focus became intentionally the unchurched: saved and unsaved. We wanted to reach both those people who had dropped out of church and those who had never had a vital relationship with Jesus Christ in the first place.

In 1995 it became abundantly clear that it was time for a Saturday evening service. By now, however, the fears from the traditional crowd had eased, and I had no one in my office wondering when I was going to cancel the traditional service. After four years of faithful ministry, they knew my commitment and understood my vision. By this time they had a sense of trust that only comes with longevity, integrity, and respect. Over the years, we had educated the people on the basic principles that would make Community Baptist both unique and effective in helping fulfill the Great Commission in Southern California. The following are our basic principles, adapted from Josh Hunt's book. These seven guiding principles gave my staff a sense of clarity in regard to our approach to ministry.

1. Quality is more important than quantity. The Lord has called us to make disciples, not merely win converts (Matt. 28:18–20; see also Col. 1:28–29). The result of our ministry should be people who increasingly hold to Jesus' teaching (John 8:31), love one another (John 13:35), and bear fruit in their lives and ministry (John 15:8).

2. Quantity is also very important. The work of the ministry should result in numerical growth as well as growth in discipleship. We should not be only strengthening and encouraging existing disciples (Acts 14:22) but making new ones as well (Acts 14:21, see also 2:41, 47; 6:1, 7; 9:31; 16:5).

3. Balance is essential for effectiveness. Specifically, disciple making requires a balance of biblical faithfulness and contemporary relevance. In other words, we must be both conservative and radical at the same time—conservative in our commitment to the Word of God, for it alone can make us wise for salvation and equipped for every good work (2 Tim. 3:15–17), and radical in our application of it (following the example of Jesus and the early church). Concerning the latter, we must be aware of the needs and cultural situation of the people in our community and be willing to sacrifice our personal preferences with respect to the nonessentials of the faith.

4. The ministry belongs to everyone. The role of the congregation is not to help the pastoral team with their ministry. Rather, the role of pastors is to equip and encourage the community of disciples in their ministry (Eph. 4:11–13). Each one of us should be reaching out to the unchurched and using our spiritual gifts to strengthen and multiply the body of Christ (Acts 1:8; 1 Peter 4:10–11). Ownership of ministry is the key to long-term motivation and effectiveness.

5. People grow best in small groups. While disciples are greatly encouraged in large group worship, most of the ministry— serving one another in love (Gal. 5:13), carrying each other's burdens (Gal. 6:2), praying for each other (James 5:16), and spurring one another on toward love and good deeds (Heb. 10:24–25)—can really only happen in small groups. Therefore we measure our success not only by participation in worship

services but also by involvement in small groups (and, it should be added, these groups should always be growing and multiplying).

6. Passion for Jesus should undergird everything. All ministry should flow out of a love relationship with Jesus Christ (1 John 4:7–11). The life of discipleship is ultimately not a matter of rules but relationship (John 1:12; 1 John 3:1–3); not duty but delight (Matt. 11:28–30; 1 John 5:3). Therefore we will place the highest value on developing and maintaining passion for the Lord above all else (Matt. 22:36–40).

7. The Holy Spirit is the best leader. Effective ministry results when we follow the leading of the Holy Spirit (Gal. 5:25; Acts 9:31). Therefore it is better to discover what the Spirit is doing and join him in it than to assume that God will bless whatever we decide to do. We discover what the Spirit of God is doing by cultivating our love relationship with the Lord (Acts 13:1–3; Eph. 5:18–21).

Gearing Up for the Harvest

Today I find myself at a new and exciting stage in the life of Community Baptist Church. The year is 1997, and by the grace of God we are officially out of space. We have an elementary school on campus that has a waiting list of students wanting a solid Christian education. Our children's ministry has exploded with the addition of another two hundred people regularly attending the 9:30 service, which is the service with the largest attendance. Our ministry to senior citizens has taken on greater priority in recent times as we not only seek to be "seeker-sensitive" but also "senior-sensitive."

With our commitment to the multiple-track approach, the concept of adding additional space for our campus was an easy one. We are not adding any dimension to the worship center other than expanding the lobby to facilitate additional fellowship. We will, though, need to add additional classroom space to meet the needs of Christian education. In addition we will have more staff offices, an expanded library, and a new bookstore.

Our theme for 1996 was "Gearing Up for the Harvest." Our desire as a leadership team was not to ask God to bless our plans, but to plan where God seemed be blessing. God is at work in the South Bay, and we're convinced he has called our church to become an active part of the pending revival coming to our land. We don't want to miss it!

Lessons I've Learned

I soon learned that wisdom can be found in learning from your own mistakes. But I have also found that there is greater wisdom in learning from the mistakes of others. Leader to leader, allow me to share the lessons I have learned in the process.

Plan carefully. We must always remember that the Lord must build his house or we labor in vain (Ps. 127:1). In your planning process establish who the new service is for. When creating any new service I found a right and a wrong reason for the change. The wrong reason, which I might add is the predominant motivation for most churches adding a service, is "we're out of room." Obviously space is a major consideration when planning for the future. But when this becomes the prime motivation for additional buildings, when a building program is finally completed, there will be people who will conclude, "Oh, finally we can all worship together again."

The correct reason to initiate this change is to reach more people for Jesus Christ. Paul said in 1 Corinthians 9:22, "To the weak I became weak, that I might win the weak. I have become all things to all men, that I may by all means save some."

Educate patiently. Always remember that people's phobias will undermine even the greatest of visions and the best of plans. Any leader who initiates this kind of paradigm shift must wrestle with the question, "Will it be worth it?" A very wise, older pastor once shared with me, "My dog can kill a skunk . . . but it's not worth the effort." In other words, you could win the battle and leave such a stink that all hopes of continued fellowship could be lost. Spend the time necessary to bring the people up to speed. This is one place where prayer will be absolutely critical to your success. Part of this process will be to ask the Lord to show you the key people with whom to share the vision. Help them come on board so they in turn can share with those they influence. If you are a new pastor, this is crucial. You usually do not yet have the necessary acceptance and/or credibility to have the more resistant types buy into the vision without someone they respect assisting them to see the value of the change.

Recruit wisely. This is an extremely important issue in the climate of quality we live in today. I have observed that sooner or later the new service is viewed as the exciting place to be, especially if the newly added service is the first one to be contemporary. Recruiting wisely simply means that we never see one service as more important than the other. We never see one service as the "varsity" service and the other as the "junior varsity" service. We desire to have gifted musicians and vocalists involved in all the services, allowing the people to choose a service because of style not quality. Remember, each service makes its own unique contribution to the family. We need to let the desirable features of each service be highlighted, so people can appreciate the particular service God leads them to attend.

Publicize attractively. The high caliber of media bombardment that surrounds every aspect of our society requires that we design publicity that will truly be attractive and read. If it doesn't catch the eye, it may well not be read. What we do for the Lord should not be of a lesser quality than what we do for ourselves or our business. If you can afford a variety of sources to communicate—print, video, drama—you will broaden your chances of having your message heard and understood.

Speak positively. God asks us to walk by faith, not by sight (2 Cor. 5:7). Faith is a positive thing. It's true there will be difficulties and problems to be faced as we accomplish our vision. But we need to see God through all we do. With him nothing is impossible. So once you know you are doing what he wants, then you can speak with confidence in positive ways about the new model. You can see him as providing the solution to any obstacles or potential obstacles that may come. If you as a staff or leadership team have reservations, you cannot expect your congregations to embrace your vision.

Pray constantly. If we are going to do anything that counts for the kingdom of God, it needs to be a part of God's design for his kingdom. That means from day one we need to be in constant contact with the Master Architect and Organizer of our church. We need to seek his will and his plans so that we can be his instruments in shaping our church into the pattern he has for us and thus fulfill the ministry to which he has called us. We need to bring him into every aspect of our planning and implementation. This is why we are told in Philippians 4:6 to pray about everything and in 1 Thessalonians 5:17 to pray continually. Prayer is not a one-time shot. It's an ongoing, powerful instrument God has given us to help us stay in the center of his will and accomplish his purposes his way with minimal mistakes.

Tragically most churches across the United States are not much of a threat to the devil. If we desire growth, we must pray. We can do all the right things, but without a firm foundation of prayer, we could miss out on the growth God intended.

Encourage unity. In John 17 Jesus prays for unity in the church. It is important that members view themselves as one body that desires the best for all rather than each looking out for his or her own interests or the interests of his or her particular part of the church. God expects and honors cooperation. The enemy is the one desiring divisions, factions, and competition. This is why the Lord warns us in Philippians 2:21 that there can be those in the church who look out for "their own interests, not those of Christ Jesus." The church that practices unity, whose members want what is best for each other, is the one God can and will bless.

A man was crawling through the desert on his hands and knees, desperate for a drink of water. He encountered a man selling neckties. "Would you like to buy a nice necktie?" asked the salesman. "All I want is a drink of water," the man growled. The salesman had no water, so the poor man kept crawling across the sand. Miraculously, out in the middle of that vast desert, he came upon a beautiful restaurant. At first he thought it was a mirage, but as he moved closer he saw that it was real. With his last ounce of energy, he struggled up to the entrance and said to the doorman, "Please, I must have a

135

drink of water." To which the doorman replied, "Sorry, gentlemen are not admitted without neckties."

Like the man who thought neckties were useless, I've learned that God may be trying to equip us in the midst of trials in ways we never consider. But he knows we (or someone else—cf. 2 Cor. 1:3ff) will need it later! Trust him! Sometimes it is only in hindsight that we understand why God allowed something. Sometimes, unlike the illustration, we never do. And that's okay because he is the Head of our church.

13

The Satellite Model

Mention the name "satellite" and people naturally think of outer space. To astronomers the name suggests the moon circling the Earth, reflecting the sun to light up the nighttime sky. To modern-day observers of the Information Age, the name brings forth thoughts of communication satellites circling the Earth, deflecting a thousand beams of information to other parts of the globe.

The satellite model is best compared to a bank that has numerous branches located in different cities. Each branch operates with some level of independence but remains corporately linked to the mother bank. Each branch enhances the others by offering services that can be accessed by more people living in different parts of the city. Each branch expands the job market by providing more opportunities for people to work. Each branch provides a measure of accountability to the others as they compare the number of transactions rendered and people served. It is one bank but in many locations. The satellite model is one church but in different locations.

Missionaries to other countries realize that the church must adapt to the culture of those they hope to reach with the gospel. The satellite model is a way for local churches to contextualize their ministry to reach people who are not willing to come to their main place of ministry. Dr. Thom Rainer writes about using a satellite model to reach new people for Christ.

> When I was a pastor in Birmingham, one of the reasons we started a satellite church was to offer a church with a contemporary worship style. One location had hymnals; the other did not. One location had a choir; the other had a praise team. One location had an organ and

piano; the other had a variety of instruments. One location had padded pews; the other had padded folding chairs.[1]

The satellite model has most often been used as a means to plant a daughter church. Dr. Elmer Towns calls this approach to church planting the "satellite principle." He defines it as "the strategy of planting churches in which the daughter churches are semi-autonomous, relating organically to the mother church and each other."[2] Dr. C. Peter Wagner adds that satellite churches "continue to have an organic relationship with the parent church. Sometimes they are called annexes or branch churches. In most cases the senior pastor of the mother or central church functions as the senior pastor of each of the satellites."[3]

While this model is a good way to plant a church, churches are discovering that the satellite model of ministry is also a superb way to expand their ministry without disturbing the traditional ministries already in place. For our understanding, satellite churches are those that have one or more worship services in locations other than the primary facility. Another term often used for satellite churches is "extended geographical parish church."[4]

Characteristics of Satellite Churches

Highland Park Baptist Church located in Chattanooga, Tennessee, pastored by Lee Roberson, and Perimeter Church located in Atlanta, Georgia, pastored by Randy Pope are two nationally known churches using a satellite model of ministry. Here are a few characteristics of this model.

Worship services in different locations. The key characteristic of a church with a satellite model of ministry is that it offers at least one additional worship service in a location away from the church's main campus (see figure 11). The multiple-track model and the satellite model are similar in that they both offer distinctive styles of church ministry to reach a variety of people. The multiple-track model, of course, offers the different styles in one location, while the satellite model offers them at different locations in a community. Churches

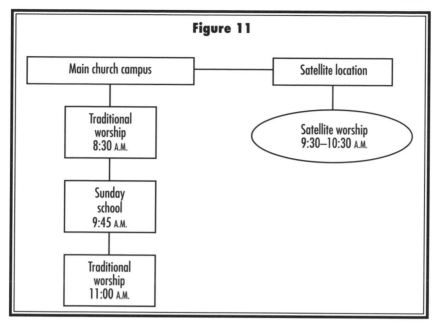

Figure 11

occasionally use facilities such as a movie theater, warehouse, another church building, or a shopping center to house the new satellite.

A different style of worship than at the main campus. It's not absolutely necessary for the satellite ministry to be a different style of worship service. For example, in the 1970s Scott Memorial Baptist Church in San Diego, California, then pastored by Dr. Tim LaHaye, was well known to be one church in two locations: Scott East and Scott West. Worship services at both locations were essentially the same style, but the two locations offered people a choice of location and facility. The main reason for creating a new satellite in many church situations, however, is to reach a different homogeneous group of people that cannot be reached through the main style of ministry. In such cases the satellite will offer a ministry with a different slant than the mother church.

Usually attracts a pioneering congregation. A different type of person is attracted to a new congregation than is attracted to an older one. People who are drawn to new ventures are most often called pioneers. They are the ones who break new ground and chart new paths for others to follow later on. One of the difficulties of an aging congregation is its inability to attract and hold on to visionary leaders. Once a congregation has been in existence for more than twenty years, it predictably will begin to exclude those people who bring new ideas and dreams for new styles of ministry. One of the characteristics of a satellite model is that it attracts and involves those who are of a pioneering spirit.

Usually takes a senior pastor with tenure. It takes a great deal of trust in the church's leaders by the members of the mother church to venture into a satellite model of ministry. For this reason churches that use this model normally have a pastor who has an above-average tenure at the church. Statistics vary depending on whom you read, but the general consensus is that the average tenure for senior pastors in the United States is less than four years. For an established church to effectively pioneer a new satellite, the pastor must be there longer than seven years.

Uses the same pastor, leaders, and budget. What makes a satellite different from a church plant is its connection to the mother church—like the branch of a bank is connected to the main office. A satellite church will have the same senior pastor who most often preaches at both locations. The same pastoral staff will service both churches, perhaps offering one ministry, like a youth program, for all the people. The offerings are collected and put into a common account, and monies are disbursed through a common budget. The main board, committees, and other administrative teams function over the entire church ministry—main campus and satellite.

Strengths of Satellite Churches

The satellite model offers many of the same strengths of the previous models with a few distinct ones. It gives an established church freedom to try something new. It is cost effective since no new facilities must be built or staff hired. Of course, the rental of an alternate facility means some increased cost. And, if it doesn't work, the church can pull it back with limited discouragement to the main body. This model has the following additional strengths.

Satellite churches meet the needs of different people. Similar to some of the other models, by offering a satellite location this model serves the interests and needs of a broader group of people. The different location may provide a means for people to attend church who might not otherwise travel to the main campus. If a different style of worship is offered, some will be attracted by the new form of worship. Others may attend due to the time of the satellite service.

Satellite churches allow for new styles of ministry to be attempted without directly affecting the main worship service. Leaders who have tried to create a new form of ministry in an established church know how difficult it can be to overcome the criticism and fear of church members. New styles of worship are resisted as people attempt to hold on to a sense of stability in a world gone mad with change. But for a church to grow and develop, new ministries must be started, and this means change must take place. One of the strengths of the satellite model is that the change can take place away from the main church campus. Church members can, and often will, give permission for a new ministry venture to be attempted somewhere else, thus protecting the established form of worship at home. It's a way to test a new idea without forcing it on the established congregation. It becomes sort of a missionary enterprise, where evangelism is done away from the main campus.

Satellite churches provide an older, ingrown church a way to fulfill the Great Commission. Studies of the life stages of congregations find that the older a congregation gets, the less effectively it fulfills the Great Commission. Churches less than three years old win people to Christ at a rate of about one new convert to every three people already in the church. In contrast, churches more than fifty years old win people at a rate of only one new convert to every eighty-seven people already in the church. The average Protestant church reaches its largest numerical size between its fifteenth and twentieth birthdays. It then levels off, conducting a worthwhile ministry for another thirty to forty years before it begins to decline in membership and ministry vitality. Adopting a satellite model of ministry allows an older, established church to fulfill the Great Commission in fresh ways so that it can continue to effectively win people to Christ as it did in its earlier years.

Satellite churches allow the mother church to make slower, less radical changes. God is surely capable of bringing renewal to older, established churches that have lost their evangelistic vitality. But, as is often the case, it takes time to bring about renewal and transformation. By using a satellite approach, the mother church can take the time to make slower changes so as not to damage the local body. If the satellite ministry proves effective, it can also serve as a model for what needs to be done at the main campus for church renewal to take place. Eventually the mother church will be enriched as new leaders emerge from the satellite church and bring new life and energy to the entire church.

Satellite churches may result in new churches. As noted earlier, the satellite model is a fine way to plant a daughter church. Church planting may not be the initial reason for starting a branch worship service, but it is possible that it may eventually grow to the point that it separates from the mother church to become a wholly independent church. This is positive and similar to a child growing up and leaving home to establish her own life and identity. The parents may be left with feelings of emptiness, but they also have great pride in the ability of their child to live on her own. Churches that choose to use a satellite approach to ministry should take great pride in a daughter church that becomes independent.

Cautions to Be Considered

The following cautions are noted for information's sake but should not be viewed as reasons to forgo starting a satellite church. The strengths of developing a new ministry far outweigh the cautions to be considered.

Satellite churches may result in the loss of a key pastor and church leaders. Occasionally the mother church may find that key leaders, even the senior pastor, may leave to join the satellite church. This occurs when the mother church has lost so much energy and ministry vitality that it cannot hold those with vision. Assertive leaders who desire to move forward will be drawn to ministries that are exciting and full of energy. If the satellite ministry exudes more spiritual vitality than the mother church, leaders will be attracted to invest their lives there rather than in the mother church at the main campus. If the satellite church becomes a separate independent church, many of the mother church's visionary leaders will jump to the satellite church, which they view as more challenging and exciting than the older established one. The challenge is to keep the mother church spiritually alive.

Satellite churches may become a threat to the main church. Church members in the established mother church may feel threatened by the satellite church. This takes place when the satellite church begins to demonstrate greater growth than the mother church. Faster growth in the satellite church is to be expected, since the satellite church is at the beginning of its life cycle, while the mother church is most likely further along in its own life cycle. While members of the mother church ought to take pride in the growth of the satellite, if they feel threatened, there may be a backlash against the satellite. In the worst case, church members may pressure the church leaders to abort the satellite project. In the best case, the satellite will be released to become an independent church.

Satellite churches may not be well represented in decisions made for the entire church. A problem occasionally arises from the greater control over the church budget and ministries exerted by the mother church. Business meetings are usually held at the main campus, meaning those who attend the satellite campus may be underrepresented during times of decision making. The larger the satellite grows and the more it donates in offerings, the more its worshipers will wish to have a voice in the overall direction of the larger church. Since the satellite is more likely to have a new model of ministry, church members at the traditional main campus may make decisions that are detrimental to the satellite.

It may be difficult to maintain a unified ministry. Church leaders will feel they are the glue that is holding the church together. If people at the main campus feel threatened, and those at the satellite campus sense they are being overlooked, great pressure will be exerted to further pull the ministry apart. Maintaining a common understanding of the purpose and vision of the church will be increasingly difficult. As long as the senior pastor remains at the church, the probability is that the vision can be directed well. But if the main visionary leaves, it will be much more difficult to keep the vision of satellite ministry alive.

There may be a tendency to grow apart over time. Even in the best of circumstances, the mother church and satellite ministry will grow apart. The natural movement of a separate group to establish its own identity will eventually take over. As the satellite depends less and less on the mother church, the satellite will move toward autonomy. Only in the case of a satellite remaining small will it tend to remain tied to the mother church over many years.

The satellite model is one approach that is being effectively used today to reach unchurched Boomers and Busters. It is particularly effective when used in an established church seeking a way to reach new people without unduly disturbing the congregation at the main campus. If the satellite model interests your church, begin by reading the study of Del Cerro Baptist Church that follows. Then visit a satellite church in your area and read chapters 5 and 10 in *10 of Today's Most Innovative Churches* (Ventura, Calif.: Regal, 1990) by Elmer L. Towns.

14

A Look at a Satellite Church

Pastor Sam Williams

Sam Williams is senior pastor of Bay Marin Community Church, 1411 Lincoln Ave., San Rafael, CA 94901, (415) 453-7959. He also is an associate professor of pastoral leadership at Golden Gate Baptist Theological Seminary, Mill Valley, California.

The purpose of Del Cerro Baptist Church is to love God and love people." On paper the new purpose statement looked rather innocuous and generic. But for a twenty-seven-year-old, plateaued, traditional church it was revolutionary. Its power was in what it meant to us, not just what it said. What it meant was that we were going to put following God before following tradition, people before programs. We were committed to reaching unchurched people and, as a church, being responsible for taking the first step toward that encounter.

The result was significant growth, which led to the development of a multiservice, multicongregation, multilocation ministry that represented one expression of what is sometimes called a satellite model of church ministry. The development of this model was partly out of necessity but mostly out of design. It represented our willingness to do what was necessary to keep reaching unchurched people for Christ, especially those who were generationally and culturally different from our existing congregation.

Del Cerro is a Southern Baptist church in the San Diego area. It had a Sunday worship attendance of four hundred when it began developing this model. From a landlocked three-acre campus with education and worship facilities for only three hundred people, we

145

developed a ministry that in a given week touched the lives of one to two thousand people at up to twelve locations in a variety of ministry styles and experiences.

A Strategic Decision

The decision to begin an off-site congregation was motivated in part by the space problems created by our growth. (We had three identical worship services with concurrent Sunday schools on Sunday morning and no more available parking.) But there was also a realization that there was a large segment of the unchurched population that we were unlikely to reach in that location with that style of ministry.

Del Cerro's worship was warm and welcoming, and the messages addressed practical needs in people's lives. But no one ever mistook the fact that we were a traditional church. The sign out front said "Baptist," the pews were padded, the choir was robed, and the windows were stained. It was good tradition, but tradition nonetheless. Because it was good, there was no reason to destroy or even weaken it. We were reaching many people who were not turned off by tradition, as long as it was not meaningless tradition.

We knew, however, that the existing facilities, name, and ministry style were not effective in reaching a generation of Boomers who had no church experience, or worse, a bad one. That was the primary reason we did not consider the alternative of making one of our Sunday morning services a "contemporary" service, or of starting a Saturday night service in our facility. Either of those alternatives would have been a logistically easier but strategically weaker decision. If we had a new target audience, we needed to develop a strategy that maximized our ability to reach it.

Crossroads Christian Community was the outgrowth of that decision. Crossroads was a separate congregation that met in a rented facility, five miles from Del Cerro's campus. Del Cerro and Crossroads shared the same vision, ministry staff, and budget. They also participated in some common events, such as singles' activities and youth camps. However, they had different worship styles, outreach strategies, ministry philosophies, and decision-making structures.

Crossroads was similar to many of the new churches targeting unchurched Boomers. It had a seeker-sensitive Sunday morning service, praise music, band, and worship ensemble. Adults met in weekday home cell groups instead of Sunday school. Direct mail and special-event Sundays were used for outreach. Structure was kept simple, and decision making was delegated to those doing ministry. I preached at Crossroads as well as at two of the three services at Del Cerro each Sunday. One staff member related primarily to Crossroads, leading worship and overseeing small groups. Other staff related in the areas of their ministry responsibility, for example, children, youth, and singles. From the beginning, Crossroads had a broad base of ministry offerings and grew quickly to more than 250 in attendance.

The growth rate at Crossroads was tempered by the next phase of our satellite ministries—new church planting. Our objective at Del Cerro/Crossroads was to reach unchurched people, not to build a large church. Strategically, we believed we could reach more people in many locations than in just one or two. In the following six years we started five new churches. Each of those churches has now become a separate congregation, but initially each was closely related to Del Cerro.

One of the limitations of satellite churches is the difficulty of the staff, especially the preaching pastor, to be present enough to identify with the congregation. Having reached that limitation with Crossroads, we hired a pastor for each of the new starts. We assumed a two-year financial responsibility for the start-up costs and the pastor's salary. The new pastor functioned as a part of our staff structure and was free to use our staff and church resources in the development of the new ministry.

We provided a core group for each start and encouraged people to consider leaving our congregations to become a part of the new churches. Proportionately more of these people came from Crossroads because its ministry philosophy was more closely attuned to that of the new starts. The significance of this, from the perspective of the satellite ministry model, is that these new churches were viewed more like "extensions" of the ministry of our church and less like "missions." People did not have to "leave" Del Cerro to be a part of the new church. They simply moved to a new part of our church's ministry. That provided a greater level of participation and started much stronger churches.

Ministry Multiplication

Once the concept of multiple ministry locations became a part of our mind-set, it led to numerous other ministry expressions. An unused church building became the location for three new congregations in an inner-city neighborhood. The three, an English-speaking congregation copastored by a Black and an Anglo pastor, a Cambodian congregation, and a Hispanic congregation, represented the racial and ethnic diversity of that neighborhood. Weekday ministries addressing the social and physical needs of the community were staffed by people from all of our congregations.

We trained lay ministry teams (preacher, worship leader, and Bible study teacher) to start congregations in convalescent homes and retirement facilities for those who were not able to leave on Sundays to go to church. The teams provided regular worship and Bible study as well as met the ongoing spiritual and ministry needs of the people who became involved. At one time we had extension congregations in three convalescent homes and two retirement complexes. A similar ministry was taking place on a nearby Indian reservation and in apartment complexes.

The number of ministries and people involved varied from time to time, but at one time, on a weekly basis, we had thirteen worship services and fifteen Bible study programs meeting in twelve different locations on six different days of the week. These were led by eight pastors and four lay pastors and involved approximately two thousand people. And while there was tremendous diversity in size and style of ministry, they were all a part of one church's vision, budget, and staff oversight.

Overall, the greatest benefit of a satellite ministry for Del Cerro was a new mind-set. We came to see the church as people, not a place, existing for ministry, not maintenance. Our church existed in all kinds of facilities, all during the week, meeting all kinds of needs.

We had escaped the physical walls of our buildings and the philosophical walls of our tradition. It was exciting and gratifying. But it had not been without its learning curve and share of mistakes, issues that I will now address and illustrate from our experience.

Getting Started

While there is no commonly accepted definition of a satellite model, for the purpose of this case study I have in mind a church that has worshiping congregations and ministries in more than one location, unified by a common vision, budget, and staff oversight.

There are varied reasons, or combinations of reasons, why churches consider the satellite model. For some it is simply a matter of providing more space for growing the existing church. Others start a satellite as a first step toward the ultimate relocation of the church, usually from a declining to a developing part of the city. The ministry decisions these churches would make would be different from the ones we made at Del Cerro. Our primary motivation was to reach people we could not reach in our present location with our existing ministry philosophy. Ours was a "mission" strategy, across generational and cultural boundaries. The principles and guidelines that follow are specific to our circumstances and reasons for developing this model, not a comprehensive look at the subject of satellite models. It is a specific case study and the lessons learned from it by those who were involved in it.

Advantages

Beyond the new mission mind-set engendered by the use of this model, there are numerous advantages to commend it. Five seem to be especially persuasive.

Satellite churches diminish the conflict over ministry styles that is tearing apart many plateaued and declining churches. The conflict is typically between older members and a pastor who wants to reach a younger generation. The result is either a broken fellowship in which no ministry style would be effective or a blended style that is not fully

149

satisfying to anyone. Establishing separate congregations allows each church to develop ministry strategies and styles that are meaningful and effective for each target audience. This is not to say that there is never any conflict, but it does not have to be faced in worship every Sunday morning.

The fellowship at Del Cerro was strengthened because our members were given ministry options to choose from, rather than being forced to choose between them. The people could go to their own kind of church. Older members of our church had a place to invite younger friends and family members who did not care for the ministry style of Del Cerro's main campus. First-time visitors who did not find their experience fully satisfying at our primary location had other options. It was about choices. The more choices we had, the more people we reached and the less conflict we experienced.

The satellite model gives each part of the church the strength of the whole. This benefit is expressed in various ways. The combined size and strength of multiple congregations generally make it possible to attract and afford more experienced and capable staff. Multiple congregations also increase the number and variety of gifts among their members that are available to the larger church. The ministry options and outreach abilities of the combined congregations are also greater than those of separate churches of the same size.

The satellite model allows the church to remain focused on ministry, not facility. Del Cerro was able to experience the benefits of an extended ministry, normally only available to large churches, without the expenditure of large sums of money for property or buildings. Money and energy normally necessary to develop property and buildings were directed toward ministry development. Our weekly ministry grew from four hundred to two thousand people without any capital expenditures. This fact was additionally attractive in reaching unchurched people who believe churches are only interested in money.

Satellite churches provide a variety of ministry options for their members. Not many laypeople, for example, have the opportunity to discover and develop church-planting skills and exercise them repeatedly. Nor are many challenged to become lay pastors and experience the fulfillment that comes from walking with people through the deep moments of their lives. The ministry options available in the typical church are teaching, singing, ushering, and serving on committees. It is not that these are meaningless, they are just too limited. Talented people need and deserve challenging ministry opportunities. The increasing challenges and needs of our ministry provided those opportunities.

Since new ministry and congregational development is inherent in the satellite model, the overall growth of the church is greater than if the church remained in one location. This fifth advantage is realized because of a well-established church-growth principle that new units grow faster than old units. Giving birth to a new congregation in a new ministry location generates excitement, involves new people, focuses prayer, and sharpens strategy in a way that week-to-week ministry in an existing church fails to do. It also requires the church to constantly call out and develop new leaders, and a church's size and strength is always proportionate to its leadership base.

In sum, we reached more people, we reached different kinds of people, we grew faster, we began more ministries, and we had a greater variety of ministries by using the satellite model than we would have had by remaining one congregation. As attractive as this model is and for all its advantages, it is not without its challenges. The satellite model is not an easy option and may be the most difficult model to establish. Its problems deserve serious consideration.

Problems

The effectiveness of this model is relative to the ability to deal with its inherent problems. Most of them are not solved once for all, but require constant attention. It is necessary to both understand the nature of the problems and be diligent in mitigating their effects. The most serious problems revolve around leadership, especially staff, because they are the ones who have the greatest interaction with the different congregations. The average member of one of our congregations was unaware of and unaffected by, and usually unconcerned about what went on in the other locations. Staff, on the other hand, dealt weekly with the following issues.

The church leadership may have difficulty embracing the big picture. This was one of the more frustrating problems for us. In principle it was relatively easy. In practice it proved elusive. The difficulty stemmed, I believe, from the fact that the leadership's ongoing ministry responsibilities required them to be narrowly focused. Strategic and resourcing decisions usually reflected their own ministry priorities rather than the larger church's. While this is a common conflict, it is multiplied when a church has multiple ministry styles and strategies.

To my surprise this was particularly a problem for our paid staff. Surprising because they were highly competent and fully committed to working as a team. We often found ourselves divided, however, because we each had our own ministry preferences. It was natural to give greater attention to the ministry location or style one liked best but it was necessary to give balanced attention to the whole. As senior pastor, I was often the only one who saw the larger issues, and it was my responsibility to constantly keep us focused on the vision.

Somewhat related to that problem was an unhealthy competitiveness between the different congregations that periodically expressed itself. Each viewed their way of "doing church" the best way and could be disparaging toward any other ministry style. It was not unlike sibling rivalry, as was our way of dealing with it. Valuing each congregation's uniqueness and giving equal praise to each one's accomplishments helped. But what proved to be most effective was having people we were reaching in the new congregations come share their testimonies with the older congregation. The effect was twofold. The new people had a greater appreciation for the commitment of the older congregation to reaching people like themselves. And the older congregation, who really wanted to reach people for Christ, got to see the result of their commitment.

Another challenge for leadership, especially staff, was the necessity to be knowledgeable about more than one way of doing ministry. The various congregations had fundamentally different ministry philosophies. It was necessary, for example, to understand that the difference between adult Sunday school classes and home cell groups was much greater than the time and place they met. Staff not only had to provide a variety of resources and kinds of training but also had to use different kinds of processes and ways of relating with the several congregations because we were dealing with several generations. That was the whole point of starting the satellite congregations in the first place and it had to be respected throughout.

Having considered some of the problems involved in this model, it might be good to remember that all ministry is difficult. Every ministry option has its problems, and none more than the option of doing nothing. In a changing and unchurched culture, that almost guarantees failure. Nothing is more difficult than watching the slow decline and death of a church.

Principles

There are many principles that are important to the success of the satellite model. In our use of it we determined at least five that are essential to its success. To ignore them is to probably fail.

Act with integrity as a leader. This ministry model is a serious step for a church to take. It's more than the latest ministry fad. Before taking it, the pastor should honestly answer three questions.

First, is the church ready to adopt this model? I had to determine whether this was simply my vision or was it God's vision for the church. I was not going to take the church kicking and screaming through this kind of change just to satisfy my ministry desires. We spent nearly a year working together to develop a vision for the kind of church we would be. When the church adopted our new vision statement, it clearly understood the changes it would entail. The ensuing process required the best of my leadership abilities, but I never led the church to do anything that it had not in principle already committed to do.

Second, is the church capable of adopting this model? Some churches may not have the size or existing lay and staff leadership to pull it off. They should not be set up for failure. Good leadership will lead them to do what they are capable of doing.

And third, am I willing to stay long enough to see the process through? I found that there were many good opportunities to leave when the difficulties and complexities of this process became apparent. But integrity required that I finish what I started. If we failed or succeeded, we would do it together.

Know what can be blended and what cannot be blended between congregations. The difficulty of reaching younger generations with traditional styles of ministry has led many churches to adopt various forms of blended worship and ministry. The satellite model is the ultimate expression of a blended ministry. It is important, therefore, to understand what can and cannot be blended. Our experience led us to three conclusions.

The first was that we could blend vision but could not blend strategy. Vision was the overall purpose and direction of the church. It's what we wanted to accomplish. Strategy was the way we did it. All of our congregations shared the same purpose statement, to "love God and love people." All shared the same five ministry objectives: (1) encounter the unchurched, (2) evangelize the lost, (3) edify believers, (4) equip disciples, and (5) extend ministers back into the world to encounter the unchurched and begin the cycle again. However, no two of our congregations accomplished their common purpose and objectives with the same strategies. Each developed ones that were effective for their unique target group.

Second, in the preaching/teaching ministry of the church, we could blend substance but could not blend style. Substance has to do with the content of the message. It cannot be compromised or changed, for it is God's Word. Style has to do with the cultural or generational preferences that determine the way the message is spoken, sung, taught, or learned. It, like strategy, needs to reflect the specific target group. In our various congregations, we had two styles of traditional ministry and at least three styles of contemporary ministry. We learned from the success of existing ministry styles, but we did not copy them from one location to another.

Finally, we determined that in the organizational structure of the church, we could blend leadership but could not blend policy. Leadership, lay or staff, can function between congregations as long as it has a missionary heart and cross-cultural skills. The policy, or decision-making structure, though, must once again reflect the uniqueness of the target group. In our congregations it varied from highly structured committees to loosely organized teams; from strong pastoral authority to widely delegated decision making. All functioned well because they were appropriate to the congregation. We could have never laid one form of policy on all the congregations.

Developing distinctive congregations is at the heart of the satellite model when it is established for mission or outreach purposes. A church that is uncomfortable with diversity would do well to choose another model.

Maintain essential organizational structure between the congregations. Satellite models have to determine what the minimal organizational structures are that bind the various congregations together as one church. We determined that the three essential elements were vision, budget, and staff. Vision and staff have been discussed already. Understanding the nature of a shared budget is equally as important.

A budget, as much as any other document, reflects the vision and ministry priorities of the church. It is the tactical document that keeps a church true to its purpose. The establishing of a satellite model requires a generous and unselfish attitude on the part of the existing congregation. We eliminated some ministries and scaled back others to develop and maintain this model. As the newer congregations grew and became more financially able, we made certain that the amount spent at each location was at least equal to the amount given there. We never wanted the smaller congregations to be financially supporting the larger, more expensive congregation. As a result, we never had conflict over finances.

Leave congregational options open. When we would start a new ministry or congregation, we never determined what its future would be. Every congregation was free to separate from the others at any time. The congregations that had their own pastors were expected to become independent of the others. The initial relationship was for the purpose of support, not control. Even the Crossroads congregation, which shared me as pastor with the Del Cerro congregation, was free to become its own church. Periodically we would give them the opportunity to reassess their own future.

This model, to be effective, cannot be about size, power, or control. It functions more from a kingdom view than from a church view.

The question it constantly asks is What will expand the kingdom? not What will make our church bigger? The church that would use it must truly believe that it is "more blessed to give than to receive," for it will give up some of its own ministries, much of its money, and many of its best leaders to the new congregations.

Understand the unique role of the founding pastor. This model of ministry, as much as any other, seems to be born out of the vision of a strong and creative leader. In part, that is one of the reasons for suggesting the first principle concerning the integrity of the leader in developing the model. On the other end, this model will likely be abandoned by the church when the founding pastor leaves. It is unusual for a church to find another pastor who shares this ministry vision and it is impossible to sustain it without the support of the pastoral leadership. This proved to be true in our own experience.

Postscript

I was the pastor at Del Cerro for twenty years, eight from the time we began developing this model. My leaving had nothing to do with the issues discussed in this chapter. It was at a time and for a reason that the church and I were both aware of before we ever initiated these changes. Knowing the close relationship between the founding pastor and this model, we tried to build in structures that would ensure its permanence but were not successful.

Not long after I left, the Crossroads congregation exercised the option that was always theirs to become a separate congregation and call their own pastor. It is a strong and growing church today. After two years of unsuccessful attempts to find a pastor who shared this vision, Del Cerro effectively abandoned it by releasing the staff member who had primary responsibility for sustaining it. By this time all of the new church plants had become self-supporting. Most of the smaller ministries are still being supported by the church. Del Cerro currently has a good pastor with a different but strong vision for the church.

How do I evaluate this experience now, from the space of three years and the events just mentioned? Obviously, any pastor would like to see his vision continue. The fact that it didn't does not change my perspective. What has happened in the past three years does not negate what happened in the previous eight. Thousands began attending church and are still active today. Many hundreds of people came to know Christ. Families were saved, relationships restored, missionaries sent, new ministries developed, and God worked in countless other ways in people's lives. Neither my leaving nor Del Cerro's subsequent decisions have changed any of that. Only our initial disobedience to follow God's leadership could have kept those things from taking place.

The Rebirthed Model

A common statement heard among church planters declares, "It is easier to give birth than to raise the dead." The intent of making such a statement is to demonstrate that it is wiser to plant new churches than to seek to raise nearly dead or rapidly declining churches to new life. Church planters have a point. When we observe physical life, it is much easier to have a baby than to raise a dead person to life. Giving birth is a natural occurrence of life. Raising the dead takes a unique act of God. Yes, it is easier to give birth than raise the dead. But the dead can be raised! Even dead churches.

We don't like to think about churches closing their doors. Yet a minimum of one-fourth of all Protestant churches in the United States are close to death, especially those with an average attendance of fewer than fifty at Sunday morning worship. Older members of such churches often hang on to memories of more healthy times of ministry. Newer members long for their church to be revitalized. If any churches are in need of a new model of ministry that will reach Boomers and Busters, it is those that are near death. Without a rebirth, most will find it increasingly difficult to exist in the coming decade, let alone have an effective ministry.

Very few concepts stimulate the mind like that of "new birth." These words remind us of the new life that is received when we put our faith in Christ. The apostle Paul declares, "Do you not know that all of us who have been baptized into Christ Jesus have been baptized into His death? Therefore we have been buried with Him through baptism into death, in order that as Christ was raised from the dead through the glory of the Father, so we too might walk in *newness of life*" (Rom. 6:3–4, emphasis mine). We must continually remind ourselves that God is in the restoration business.

The resurrected life of Jesus Christ resides in each and every believer. Since believers make up the church, the new life of Christ resides in every local assembly. In Revelation 2:5 God speaks to the church in Ephesus about returning to its first love, "Remember therefore from where you have fallen, and repent and do the deeds you did at first." The power to renew itself already resided in the church at Ephesus, as it does in each and every church in existence today through the resurrection power of Jesus Christ. Throughout the years church leaders have often spoken of this possibility for church restoration as renewal or revival. One of the new models of church ministry being used today is the rebirthed model. Rebirthed churches are those that are restored to new life and vitality by ceasing to use one form of ministry and replacing it with an alternate form of more effective ministry.

Perhaps the most common approach to rebirthing a church takes place as follows. First, an established church comes to recognize that the form of the present ministry is not working. Indeed, the church may be approaching the end of a slow decline that has jeopardized the church's financial integrity. Second, a small core of people envision a new future for the church. Third, through a series of events and meetings, the church agrees to close its public ministry and release current members to join other churches or commit to becoming part of a new direction for the church. Legal status, such as state corporation, is not closed out but kept active so that the rebirthed church can burst forth with a new public ministry later on. Appropriate legal changes, such as a new church name, are made as needed to the old corporation. Fourth, following a six- to twelve-month cocooning phase, during which plans for a new church are prayerfully formulated, the church rebirths itself onto the public scene as a new church.

Characteristics of Rebirthed Churches

The rebirthed model usually arises from a prognosis of decline and potential church closure, and thus the characteristics of rebirthed churches are different from those of the others.

Rebirthed churches usually were very small. As one might expect, churches that go through a total rebirth usually were quite small. Memories of effective ministry in years gone by provided the main source of corporate self-esteem. Larger churches sense no need to go through a rebirth since their ministry continues to reach enough new people to keep the church healthy. Churches larger than two hundred have enough strength to develop one of the other models already mentioned in previous chapters. Churches averaging fewer than two hundred in worship will be most open to a rebirth. Even among them, it is usually churches with fewer than fifty at the main morning worship service who are serious candidates for a rebirth.

Rebirthed churches generally were ineffective in ministry. The smaller a church becomes, the more difficult it is for it to provide any semblance of effective ministry. A lack of attendance often leaves the church with such a small mass of people that the worship service feels hollow. A loss of funds due to limited giving units results in less money to resource outreach. Older congregations may face deteriorating neighborhoods and facilities with no ability to refurbish them to attract the new generations desiring a higher quality of ministry. While these churches do serve some members, they inherently understand that their days are numbered if something doesn't change. However, they may deny the signs of decline for many years before taking action.

Rebirthed churches usually have a core group of people who have a vision for a new style of ministry. Amidst the declining attendance, deteriorating facilities, and reduced capacity for ministry, a core group of people existed with a vision for renewed growth. The core may be as small as six or eight people or as large as fifty to seventy-five. It is an absolute fact that for a church to be rebirthed, there must be a core of people who have the vision and passion to see it take place.

Rebirthed churches usually have a senior pastor with a vision for a new style of church, perhaps with a church-planting background. The senior pastor absolutely must be a part of the core visionary group. Otherwise a new pastor will need to be called to give leadership and shape to the vision. In many cases, the senior pastor is well versed or experienced in church planting. At the heart of the rebirthed model is the replanting of a church within a church. The same skills needed to plant a church are most often called for in rebirthing a church.

Rebirthed churches usually experienced a sense of desperation. Without question, the main driving force behind most rebirthed churches was an overwhelming sense of desperation. Members and leaders in the church realized that something had to be done or the church would close its doors. Defining desperation in practical terms is difficult, but taken as a whole, the following are the major indicators that a church should seriously consider rebirthing. The more they reflect the church, the more the church needs to be rebirthed.

1. *Public worship attendance.* A church needs at least fifty adults to have a public worship service that is celebrative and attractive to new people. Twenty to forty adults at worship make the church appear unhealthy. Fewer than twenty adults is a strong indication the church should be rebirthed.
2. *Total giving units.* It usually takes a minimum of ten to twelve faithful giving units to provide for a full-time pastor. It takes another ten to twelve units to provide for the ministry of a church in terms of supplies, advertising, and basic ministry. A church reaches a danger point when it has twenty-five or fewer giving units.
3. *Lay leadership pool.* As a rule of thumb, a church needs one leader for every ten adult members (junior high and up), one leader for every six elementary school children, and one leader for every two children below school age. Fewer leaders than this will make it difficult to provide for the needs of a growing ministry.
4. *An effective ministry.* A church needs at least one ministry for which it is known in the community. For example, some churches may be known as the church with the great Sunday school, others for their children's program. A church without a clear identity may need to be rebirthed.
5. *Declining growth rate.* A growth rate that has been declining for five to ten years should serve as a warning signal. If a church is only about one-fourth or less of its original size, it is likely to be facing hard times that may result in closure if rebirthing does not take place.

6. *Congregation's spiritual health.* A church's spiritual climate is another factor to be considered. Is the church characterized by its peace, happiness, and love? Or is it filled with anger, bitterness, and discouragement?

7. *Average membership tenure.* How long have people been attending church? If the average membership tenure is longer than twenty years, it is a sign that a church is having difficulty reaching and assimilating new people. In a location with high mobility, an average tenure of more than ten years will be too long.

8. *Focus on goals.* Is the church focused in on itself or out on new people? Do leaders talk about ministry, mission, and purpose? Or do they talk about paying the bills, hanging on, real estate, the past, and member care? If the goals of a church are mostly focused inward, the church may need a new birth.

9. *Budget expenditures.* Where is the money invested? Is it invested in outreach, advertising, and ministry? Or are these items the first to be cut when the budget is tight? If a church is experiencing major cutbacks in ministry, it is a sign it needs to be rebirthed.

10. *Church rumors.* Is there positive talk about God and his work in the church? Are there people who believe God can renew the church in the days ahead? Or do people talk exclusively about the past, respond pessimistically to visionary statements, and fail to recognize that God is at work in their church? When church members look to the past for corporate self-esteem, a reb irth is probably needed.

It is estimated that in the United States between three and four thousand churches close their doors each year. An additional thirty to forty thousand are on the pathway to closure within the next decade if they do not establish a new direction in ministry. These churches should consider the possibility of rebirthing in their existing locations for continued vitality in fulfilling the Great Commission.

Strengths of the Rebirthed Model

Examples can be found of strong churches that were once nearly dead but experienced a rebirth. The Church on the Way in Van Nuys,

California, pastored by Dr. Jack Hayford, and Calvary Church of Westlake Village, California, pastored by Dr. Larry DeWitt are two well-known examples.

They have vision. It takes great faith and vision to close the doors on a dying ministry in the hope of opening up a newer, improved one. No one wants to shut down any ministry that has faithfully served God through the years. Yet there is a great difference in closing forever and closing to reopen. The first is regrettable; the second is visionary. The first takes no faith; the second requires faith. The first removes a testimony to God's work; the second creates a more effective testimony.

They serve as an example of God's renewing work. God is in the business of restoring lost men and women to himself. His creative work continues to be demonstrated every time a person receives him as Lord and Savior. In a similar manner, God's power to restore is revealed in a local body of believers pulled back from the edge of desperation to a new ministry.

They result in better use of facilities, money, and people. Churches on the brink of closing down honestly are not very good stewards of the resources God has granted them. By redirecting resources that are no longer being used well, rebirthed churches discover more promising ministries and programs that reach new people for Christ. Often this means selling property and relocating to new areas where a church can begin with a fresh vision. It always means the elimination of treasured programs from yesteryear and the investing of time, energy, and money into new ways to reach out to new generations who need Christ as much as previous ones.

They usually reopen with a much larger attendance than the previous congregation. Once a church determines to rebirth itself, it gains new energy and focus. As the core leaders dream, strategize, and plan for a new church, new life emerges that attracts new people to the new church. The spirit is reminiscent of a new church plant. People are drawn to the new church to be in on the ground floor of the new enterprise. The result most often is more people attending the new church than the former one.

They have increased enthusiasm and flexibility for new ministry. After years of effective ministry, established churches fall into the trap of repeating ministries even when they no longer are effective. It is nearly impossible to crawl out of such a repetitive rut to create newer forms of ministry capable of reaching new generations of people. By rebirthing a new church out of the ashes of an older one, the opportunity for attempting new ways to reaching out can be used. This new of flexibility brings about a fresh enthusiasm for church growth.

Cautions to Be Considered

The decision to rebirth a church should be approached cautiously but in faith, realizing that God is capable of renewing any church that is willing to change.

The church may not reopen. A major issue to be considered is the fact that once a church closes, it may not reopen, due to a number of circumstances. It is possible that the core group will not bond together as well as originally expected. If the small, fragile core group disintegrates, a stillbirth rather than a rebirth may result.

The closing may be a threat to the denomination because of the loss of a church and money. A church that is part of a denominational structure may also face criticism for closing its doors even though it plans to reopen. Denominational leaders voice concern over a lost source of revenue for denominational programs. If a local assembly sells its property, additional concern will be expressed over control of the resulting funds. If you consider using a rebirthed model, be sure to talk it over at length with denominational leaders, taking care to get their approval and support. In some cases it will be wise to ask for permission in writing, so that you spell out the length of time your church has to accomplish its rebirthing goal before the denominational leadership steps in to take over.

Fear of real estate and building costs may inhibit the rebirth. I've found that future property and building costs tend to stall the move toward rebirthing a church. This is especially true when an established church feels it should sell its present property and facilities. The fear is that the higher costs of purchasing land and building facilities at today's rates are too expensive for the rebirthed church to overcome. While costs for such items are high in today's economy, such concern should not be an obstacle. The greatest obstacle to growth is the lack of vision. When a church has the vision, it can accomplish much. Many churches are being planted in our expensive economy, and a rebirthed church with renewed vision and energy will be able to accomplish much more than a dying established church.

When the money is not carefully controlled, problems may develop. Care must be exercised to handle all monies with integrity, especially when large funds result from the sale of a building or property. In most states the funds derived from the sale of property and facilities belonging to nonprofit corporations may not accrue to the benefit of a single individual or group of individuals. Thus church leaders should be extremely diligent to protect such funds in a fiscally responsible manner.

When it takes too long to rebirth the new church, people lose the vision. Once a rebirth begins in earnest, it is best if the new church goes public within twelve months. The trick is to go public before you lose the momentum of the core group but not before the church is able to accomplish an effective rebirth.

Is the Rebirthed Model for You?

If you are faced with a church you think should possibly consider rebirthing, the following questionnaire may prove helpful in giving you an objective evaluation.

Circle YES or NO for each question.

1. Does your church have an average public worship attendance of more than 50 adults?   YES   NO

2. Does your church have 25 faithful giving units, each giving a minimum of 10 percent of their total income to your church?   YES   NO

3. Does your church have at least one competent lay leader for every 10 adults?   YES   NO

4. Does your church have at least one ministry for which it is well known in your community?   YES   NO

5. Does your church have a positive growth rate over the past 10 years?   YES   NO

Is the Rebirthed Model for You? *(continued)*

6. Does your church demonstrate a healthy spiritual life? YES NO

7. Does your church have an average membership tenure of less than 10 years? YES NO

8. Does your church talk mostly about its future goals of ministry? YES NO

9. Does your church spend at least 5 percent of its total budget on outreach to the local community? YES NO

10. Does your church have hope that God can renew its growth and vitality in its current situation? YES NO

Add the YES answers.

7–10 YES answers is excellent! This is a church with great potential.

4–6 YES answers is fair. This is a church with unclear direction. It may grow or decline.

1–3 YES answers is poor. This is a church with a limited future, and it should be rebirthed.

The rebirthed model is especially helpful for churches that are in desperate situations following several years of decline. Rather than closing their doors of ministry forever, rebirthing into a new form of ministry should be seriously considered. If you sense that the rebirthed model is for your church, begin by reading the study of Bay Horizons Church that follows. Then visit a church in your area that has been rebirthed and interview its pastors and leaders to learn how they did it. Read *To Dream Again* (Nashville: Broadman & Holman, 1981) by Robert Dale.

16

A Look at a Rebirthed Church

Pastor Jim Meyer

Jim Meyer is senior pastor of Bay Horizons Church, 2880 Bowers Avenue, Santa Clara, CA 95051, (408) 748-7330, FAX (408) 748-9318.

It was one of the worst days of my life. The church I'd pastored for the previous three years had just celebrated its third anniversary, but the day was poorly organized, attendance fell well below expectations, and morale was low. It was hard to admit it, but our church was failing. At the age of thirty-two, I had a beautiful wife, two healthy children, and a relatively secure job, but I lacked one thing: a growing and fulfilling church ministry.

There was every reason to believe I would become a successful pastor. Ministry roots ran deep in my family. My grandfather and father were both pastors, as were my stepfather and father-in-law. I had served as a youth pastor in three churches, and God blessed those ministries with spiritual and numerical growth. But after graduating from seminary and completing ordination, I lost my zeal for youth work. Instead, I wanted to pastor a church. A colleague advised me to take the first church available, so I accepted a call to a small church in Sunnyvale, California, at the age of twenty-seven.

Two Unique Church Situations

The congregation was largely composed of adults over sixty years of age who didn't feel at home in any other church. The leadership had fired their previous pastor, and I was the fourth pastor in their brief five-year history. Services were held in a rented school cafeteria, and guests had to navigate a maze of residential streets to find it. Worship services were very traditional (organ and piano) and tinged with old-time gospel music. My charter was to attract younger couples and ensure the church's future.

After two years there were as many people under thirty as there were over sixty, but growth brought tensions over music style, dress standards, and commitment levels. When a doctrinal dispute suddenly arose, the deacons initially backed my leadership, then withdrew their support when a key family threatened to leave. I felt betrayed and wanted to resign but I played it safe and stayed while actively seeking another pastorate.

During this time I became friends with the assistant pastor of our sister church in nearby Santa Clara. Over weekly breakfasts he told me about his church's plateaued growth and fading finances. I told him about our doctrinal conflict and the impending expiration of a school lease. A short time after our conversation he called to let me know that his church was interested in discussing a possible merger between our two churches. Our church would gain a permanent facility and a younger mind-set, while his church would gain an influx of believers and enough funds to retire their debt. It sounded good, but we both agreed the proposal was fraught with land mines. I didn't want to pastor a merged church, since my research indicated that most mergers ended in failure. But the Sunnyvale and Santa Clara churches merged, and I agreed to pastor the newly formed Homestead Baptist Fellowship Church.

In the euphoria of merger mania, Homestead initially prospered. I spent a lot of time trying to cultivate relationships between the two groups. Though the church lacked a sanctuary and held services in its social hall, we hoped to convert our compact gymnasium into a worship center. The facility had been debt-free for five years. However, seventeen months after we began, the merger unraveled. The leaders from the Sunnyvale church, who were used to a more traditional ministry, became increasingly distrustful of the Santa Clara leaders, who sought to be more progressive. Within a few months, twenty-five key leaders from the Sunnyvale church left in bitterness. The Homestead Baptist Fellowship Church never recovered.

During the next eighteen months entire ministries died slow, painful deaths. We were forced to let our youth pastor go, which gradually killed the youth group, and when our choir director left, the choir collapsed as well. No matter what we tried, we couldn't seem to stop the downward spiral. I read the latest church growth books and consulted with Christian leaders. The elders and I attended growth seminars and went away for overnight retreats. All that we learned led to a flurry of activity over the next few years. We created a new purpose statement and published annual goals. We revised the constitution, restructured the church around an elder board, and rescheduled our services. We remodeled the social hall where we held services, repainted the entire facility, and raised money for a new sign. We held special prayer nights, began a children's ministry, embraced an outward-focused evangelism strategy, and even tried a few outreach events. On top of that, we slowly modernized our Sunday worship service. A group of young men started a praise band, and we made subtle changes in our service. We worked hard at upgrading the quality of our ministry and became a healthier church, but no matter what we tried, we couldn't seem to grow. When our entire seniors Sunday school class left to start another church, we wondered how long Homestead could survive. And when we finally enjoyed a brief growth spurt, 25 percent of our regular attendees suddenly moved from the area within six months. It was time to face some painful facts.

Our church had existed on the same site for almost thirty-five years. We owned our 1.8 acres free and clear. And yet over time, we had settled into a comfortable mind-set. Our social hall felt full with seventy people. We had enough of an income stream to survive indefinitely. But because we were losing more people than we were gaining, we weren't having any impact in our community. We tried everything we knew, but nothing worked. It was time for a different approach.

The Rebirthing Process

After six years of relatively unproductive ministry, I needed some objective counsel. I asked a respected pastor friend if he would visit me and share his opinion of our prospects. I'll never forget the day we stood in front of our freshly painted facility and he said, "I wouldn't come here." He pointed out that our facility was cramped, oddly structured, almost invisible from the street, and made a poor first impression. Though we had researched the costs of converting our gym into a sanctuary, what would change if we did? Our facility by itself wasn't our biggest problem but it seemed to stifle any vision. We needed to do more than just make cosmetic changes. We didn't know exactly what we should do but we knew we had to take a risk.

During mornings that fall, I walked through my neighborhood and talked to God, using the Lord's Prayer as an outline. When I got to the request, "Thy will be done," I told God that I was unhappy and could only see five options for my future: stay as pastor at Homestead, pastor another church somewhere else, become an assistant pastor, begin a marketplace career, or sell the church property and start over. Even though I preferred to pastor another church, I told God that since he knew best, I'd do whatever he told me to do.

It's amazing how God guides his children. I was now thirty-six years old and had been in church ministry for fifteen years. I had entered ministry with some lofty goals, but God had allowed every dream to be crushed. I felt hemmed in, so broken inside that I was willing to follow wherever God led. He was doing something, but I didn't know what it was. Slowly he began to show me.

One day the next January I drove to the East Bay city of Pleasanton for a regular lunch date with some pastor friends. As I shared my current frustrations with the group, John Merritt, who pastored a young seeker-centered church, blurted out, "Jim, why don't you sell your church and start over!" I initially shrugged off John's suggestion but mentally filed it away.

A few weeks later, another pastor friend called to tell me about a seminar he had attended featuring Pastor Bill Hybels from Willow Creek Community Church near Chicago. He had bought the seminar tapes and encouraged me to listen to them. I initially resisted. I had never heard Bill Hybels speak but after reading some articles he'd written, I thought he sounded like a high-powered, self-promoting yuppie. But my friend insisted I was wrong, and I finally agreed to listen to the tapes. I'm glad I did. They literally changed my life.

Rather than sounding arrogant, Bill Hybels came off like a broken man. I could tell that he too had been crushed in ministry. As he talked about how his church's seeker-centered ministry originated, I readily identified with a number of things he said, especially his desire to reach unchurched people—a dream I had long buried.

I had a Sunday off, so my wife, Kim, and I decided to visit the seeker service at Cross Winds Church, where my friend John Merritt pastored. I was impressed by its excellence, relevance, thematic-structure, and electric atmosphere. But I was even more blown away by all the spiritual seekers who attended. As the service progressed, I told myself, "We can do what they're doing!" Later that day, Kim and I drove along the coast and brainstormed how Homestead could become a church that reached unchurched people for Jesus Christ. The more we talked, the more excited we became. We placed our lives in God's hands and felt much more hopeful about the future.

God was doing a powerful work in my life. While preaching a series of messages on Hebrews 11, I was struck by how God told Noah to build an ark for a coming flood, even though Noah had never seen either one. I asked myself, "Could God be asking me to do something without much precedent?" Even though I'm used to playing it safe, God was using my discontent, John Merritt's comment, Bill Hybels's tapes, the Cross Winds service, and the series on faith to prepare me to take a risk for him. And I believed that risk involved selling our church property and starting a new church. But how would I sell this vision to the elders?

Rather than approach them collectively, I decided to approach the four of them individually. After reviewing our church's history and future prospects, I told them what God was doing in my heart. I asked them to pray about the possibility of selling our church property and beginning a new church in a different location that could reach unchurched people for Jesus Christ.

Wendell, the chairman of our board, could have stopped the whole process. He had dreams of a sanctuary on Homestead's front lawn and a few church buildings were already named for his family members. But he joined with George, the other senior elder, and told me, "We failed to reach our generation for Christ but we want to do everything possible so you can reach yours." The same God who was working in my heart was also working in theirs. Richard and Roger, the two younger elders, eagerly embraced the vision as well.

Soon we met as a group and formalized our decision by hammering out this charter:

> To begin a new church with a new name in a new location in Santa Clara, funded primarily through the proceeds from the sale of our present property, to reach unchurched people for Jesus Christ.

We agreed to lease a light industrial building rather than buy land and to hire two new staff members. God had convinced us to start a new church. But how would we convince the church body? We put together a presentation detailing our church's past, recent history, and future vision. We rehearsed it, tried to anticipate objections, set a date for an informational meeting, and encouraged every regular attender to be there. At the same time, I began consulting with non-elder opinion makers about our proposal.

When we finally made our presentation to the congregation in May 1990, there was an understandable mixture of enthusiasm and shock. We told our people that due to the emotional nature of the meeting, we wouldn't vote or entertain any public comments, which they might later regret. But we did announce that we would hold a series of five home meetings so they could ask questions or voice concerns. I made sure to attend each meeting, along with various elders. We also encouraged our people to submit written questions to us and to visit the Cross Winds Church in Pleasanton to witness a seeker ministry. Seven weeks after our initial presentation, the church body voted thirty-two to seven in favor of our new vision. We did lose two families who had recently joined our church, but they left amiably and wished us well.

Since we wanted to hold the first service in our new church on March 17, 1991 (one month before Easter), we had to move quickly in the intervening nine months. So that we could maintain unity without the stress of endless meetings and potentially divisive votes, the elders received empowerment from the church to choose a new name, sell the property, find a facility to lease, and disburse church possessions. We promised to consult the church every step of the way.

Looking back, I can see how God prepared us to start a new church:

- I'd pastored what felt like a sinking ship for six and a half years but along the way I had earned trust as a leader who didn't run when things got tough (even though I felt like running many times).
- Our church lacked the necessary critical mass to break through attendance barriers and attract a wider population segment but we were large enough to make a great core group for a new church.
- Even though many of Homestead's ministries collapsed, that gave us the freedom to experiment with new ministries, which made the transition to a seeker ministry much smoother.
- Because most of our seniors had left us, moved away, or died, the church gradually became composed of young families who grew into owning the ministry with enthusiasm.
- Though our property seemed like a liability to our vision, it became an asset when we thought about selling it.
- Even though my ministry dreams and those of our board chairman had been snuffed out, from the ashes God brought us a whole new set of dreams.
- For years we had thought small and played it safe, but God made us desperate enough that we felt it was time to think big and take a risk for Christ's kingdom.

The church's morale improved overnight. Rather than being haunted by past failures, we realized our whole future lay ahead of us. True, in many ways we seemed like the same people, but God was doing a deep work in our lives. Because of his impeccable timing, we were living a miracle.

How the Rebirth Took Place

During the next several months, our elders held countless lunch and evening meetings. We viewed our new church as a once-in-a-lifetime venture, so we wanted to make the best possible decisions. In the back of our minds, we believed God was giving us a second chance and we didn't want to disappoint him.

We made careful plans to sell the property, invest the funds wisely, locate and lease a facility, purchase new equipment and furniture, hire two staff members, and train the congregation for a seeker-centered ministry. We had to close down one church, open another one, and run an existing church simultaneously. Looking back, I get exhausted just thinking about how unrealistic we were to believe we could complete all of that within nine months. But at the time, we thought we could do anything. We formed ministry teams for staff, a new site, marketing, finance, furnishings, and technology. All the teams reported to the elders.

Meanwhile, the marketing team drove the process of choosing a new church name. After asking the congregation for suggestions, we set up an evaluation criteria and settled on three possibilities. After surveying the preferences of unchurched people, someone suggested combining two of the three names together, and we agreed to call our new ministry Bay Horizons Church. The marketing team worked tirelessly on interpreting demographic studies, as well as creating a logo, brochure, direct mail piece, and new sign.

Having grown up in Christian circles, I heard very little about the power of a vision statement. But the best thing our marketing team did was hammer out this twenty-five-word statement for Bay Horizons:

> To become a regional church that effectively presents the gospel of Jesus Christ with integrity, creativity, and excellence so that spiritual seekers become faithful disciples.

That God-given vision, regularly expounded to our people, has created a unity and a passion that I have never experienced in any other church.

During this time our relocation team was scouting out possible church sites in our city's light industrial area. Our criteria included street visibility, easy accessibility, plenty of parking, room for expansion, and a high ceiling for multimedia presentations. In the summer of 1991, after looking at more than thirty-five sites, we signed a temporary lease and surrendered our old church property to the Salvation Army. We also had to decide what to do with the church's possessions. We sold some items, gave away or tossed others, and moved what we could use to our new site.

Our core group began holding services in an upstairs room that barely held one hundred people. Downstairs, workmen were renovating a large warehouse into an auditorium, tearing down and rebuilding walls, and doing seismic upgrading. Because the city wouldn't let us meet in our converted warehouse until we obtained our temporary occupancy permit, we kept setting new grand opening dates. In fact, we set seven of them before we finally opened up. Being assured by our contractor that we would have our temporary occupancy permit in early October 1992, we had scheduled a Christian rock concert for a Sunday evening, October 11. But in early October, without obtaining our needed permit, the contractor walked off the job. We didn't believe God had led us this far to fail, but humanly speaking, we felt like giving up. Here it was, twenty-eight months after we'd decided to start Bay Horizons, and we still weren't open! As we had done so many times before, we committed our church to God. In the midst of our most severe financial shortages, God quietly but clearly spoke to my anxieties during a worship service. He said, "Jim, you take care of the ministry, and I'll take care of the money." He has tested my faith many times concerning finances but he has never let us down.

Somehow, without time to spare, we obtained our temporary occupancy permit about 5:00 P.M. on Friday, October 9. We held our first service with our core group in our spacious but carpetless new auditorium on October 11, and that night, four hundred people packed the place for an incredible concert. I was thrilled that God had performed another miracle! We put all our long-ready marketing plans into action and finally held our grand opening service on November 8, 1992. On that rainy Sunday, 311 people attended Bay Horizons' first celebration service.

All during this time, I felt an incredible sense of frustration. I had never been trained to deal with contractors or money managers or building owners before yet I felt I had to learn if our church was going to survive. I spent all my waking hours trying to figure out how to raise the funds to keep us afloat. Week after week, I wondered if we'd be able to pay our rent and our bills, but by God's grace, we always did. Looking back, we'd definitely do things differently the next time. When people asked me how the church was going, I'd say, "The ministry end is going great. The business end stinks." But business issues aside, Bay Horizons has been the most exciting ministry I've ever known.

Bay Horizons' Ministry

Since we opened in November 1992, God has performed miracle after miracle at Bay Horizons. Many adults have come to faith in Christ. We enjoy a steady stream of guests. Our leadership team is spiritually strong and relationally healthy. Our current staff of four includes three people who have full-time marketplace jobs yet work part-time for us. We've lost very few people from our original core group and have stayed united around our vision to see "spiritual seekers become faithful disciples." We aren't perfect and we have a long way to go in many areas, but it's exciting to be a part of a church that's making a difference.

Trained as an expository preacher, I've learned how to give application-oriented messages on Sundays, which I enjoy very much. It's thrilling to speak to people who are hungry to know God. I talk freely about any and all topics from Scripture, including sin, judgment, hell, and moral and social issues. I never cease to be amazed at how receptive people are to God's truth. Leading and teaching Bay Horizons has become so fulfilling and fruitful for me that I can't imagine doing anything else.

We've already seen more adult conversions at Bay Horizons than in any church I've ever attended. This past fall, so many of our seekers came to Christ that we needed an influx of unbelievers just to keep Sunday morning seeker centered! Our people continue to befriend unchurched people and invite them to our Sunday service.

The people who serve at Bay Horizons are so passionate about their ministries that I don't have to push them—but sometimes I have to force them to go home! My whole family enjoys serving as well. My wife, Kim, has started many ministries and is currently our children's director. Our seventeen-year-old son, Ryan, runs the sound ministry, and our fourteen-year-old daughter, Sarah, teaches children. Kim has invited scores of her coworkers to our church, and some have stayed and received Christ. While still in fifth grade, Sarah invited so many friends that at one time, five of their families were attending our church and some have committed their lives to Jesus.

What I've Learned

On his initial visit to our church, my brother John attended a Thursday night rehearsal where more than twenty-five people were present. He was so impressed he told me, "Jim, you're lucky to be a part of a church like this." I know what he meant, but it's not luck. It's the grace of God. In the entire process I've learned a great deal.

First, I learned that I had to face reality. No matter how much I convinced myself otherwise, our lack of a sanctuary would always hurt us. And even if we put one up, it wouldn't give us a matching vision. We looked like a minor-league operation to guests, and we felt minor league ourselves. The church that eventually bought our property did put up a sanctuary and has spent hundreds of thousands of dollars renovating the property, but they've grown very little.

Because I was emotionally involved with our church's ministry, I couldn't step back and objectively look at our future. I needed to ask some outside experts to tell me the truth, and when they did, it hurt. Our church was dying, and we were in denial about it. Only when we faced the cold hard facts together did we consider necessary big-picture options. We needed to birth a new baby.

In many churches veteran board members and leaders often block the pastor's attempt to have a relevant and effective ministry. But in our situation, Wendell and George, who had each been in the church more than twenty-five years, were willing to lay down their own dreams and ambitions so we could reach younger generations for Christ. They could have shut the project down before it ever started but they didn't and instead led the charge, for which I will be eternally grateful.

Second, I've learned that a church needs a well-defined, largely owned vision to prosper. The first two churches I pastored lacked any sense of vision, and because of that, we all had different agendas. I had a vague mental picture of the kind of church I wanted, as did those in leadership, but we never had the same picture. Because of that, there was always conflict simmering under the surface.

But today, that's all changed. Our vision of seeing "spiritual seekers become faithful disciples" drives our whole ministry. All our leaders not only know what our vision is, they can also explain it to others. When God gives his people a vision, it motivates them so that the pastor doesn't have to preach nearly as many "get committed" messages. An "expert" once told me he doubted we could make our new church work "with that group you've got there," but he didn't know how hard we were willing to work. Only God knew.

Third, I've learned that at some time every church needs to take a risk for God. Many Christian leaders don't want to take risks because they're afraid they'll lose some people or split their church or lose their job or even ruin their career. But as I study Scripture, whether it was David facing Goliath, Elijah on Mount Carmel, or Paul planting new churches, those who took the greatest risks were the ones who witnessed the greatest miracles. Because our church was dying, what did we have to lose by taking a risk? I have found that God delights in honoring those who trust in his promises. No obstacles, no miracles!

Fourth, I've learned that the process is as important as the product. One of the smartest things we did during the rebirthing process was to explain and re-explain to our church exactly where we were headed and why. We never assumed that people would understand new ideas the first time. We held many all-church meetings to share the latest news and to dialogue openly with our church, but we never voted on anything at those informational meetings. If we did need to vote on an issue, we would hold two meetings: an informational meeting to present and discuss the issue without using Robert's Rules of Order and a brief business meeting the next week that did use Robert's Rules. Not surprisingly, informational meetings have always been well attended, while business meetings have not. I am convinced that people want their say more than their way. This two-pronged approach to meetings, while somewhat time-consuming, has kept our church united during incredibly stressful times.

Fifth, I've learned that as we honor God, God honors us. Countless times over the past fifty-eight months, I wondered if we'd have enough money to pay our rent and keep our church in operation. And countless times, we've gone to God in prayer, and he's always come through. As I write this in February 1996, we're only one month away from being debt-free. Our trust isn't in the almighty dollar, but in almighty God. I couldn't have said this ten years ago at Homestead's anniversary celebration, but if I died tonight, I would leave this earth satisfied that I had fulfilled God's purpose for my life.

17

Remodeling Your Church

An old adage assures us that, "A new broom sweeps clean." If you are a church leader exploring the potential of using a new model of church ministry, you are the new broom. In your efforts to facilitate a new model of ministry, you will be attempting to sweep your church clean or to shake things up, get the church moving, implement changes.

But why go to all the trouble of installing a new model of ministry? The only valid reason is to create a more effective ministry to Boomers and Busters. No doubt a large majority of your Builders are fairly pleased with your church's current ministry. If they were the only generation you were concerned about, there would be no need to develop a new model. If your church wishes to make disciples of Boomers and Busters, however, you may need a new model to be most effective.

At this point you may be tempted to implement a new model of ministry in as little time as possible. Your passion is admirable but remember that there are often hazards that must be removed or avoided before you can proceed. Dangers may hide below the surface like rocks in a river, unseen but capable of harming unwary travelers on the surface. How do you lead your church to adopt a new model of ministry without losing your sanity? Or, in the case of a pastor, your job?

Questions to Ask before You Start

Take the time right now to consider the following eight questions before you stir up church leaders and members of the congregation with dreams of a new model of ministry.

What is your purpose? Review the purpose of your church. What are you trying to accomplish through your ministry? If your church lacks an up-to-date statement of its purpose, work with key leaders to develop a new one. Your purpose statement should be less than twenty-five words in length, so that it can be communicated easily. Take the time to communicate your purpose to the entire church constituency, as it gives you the biblical reason for developing a new model of ministry.

Is your present model of ministry accomplishing your purpose? Ask your leaders to compare the purpose statement with what they are doing. Put together several working teams (not committees) and ask them to evaluate your church against your purpose statement. Honestly evaluate the extent to which you are fulfilling your God-given purpose. If you find that your present model of ministry accomplishes your purpose, there may be no need to begin another model of ministry. Obviously if your purpose is not being reached, consideration should be given to selecting a new model of ministry that will be more effective. However, even if your church is fulfilling its purpose, some models of ministry, such as satellite or multiple-track, may still be appropriate as a means to expand your ministry.

Who are you trying to reach? Begin by determining who you are as a church. While the current makeup of your congregation should not be an excuse for failure to reach out to those unlike you, it does limit to some extent who you can reach effectively today. Once you know who you are, develop a population profile of the people in your ministry area. Obtain good demographic information showing exact percentages of different groups of people in your area. Then:

- Discover the felt needs of unchurched people in your community.
- Learn the fears or stereotypes that keep them from attending church.
- Assume that God is working in their lives and that some would come to church if their fears and needs were addressed by your church.
- Take the initiative to develop a new model of ministry that will effectively reach these people for Christ.

Which new model would facilitate a more effective ministry? Of the six models of ministry discussed in previous chapters, which appears to be the most appropriate for your church? Would any specific model be easier to implement than others? Which one would be the best approach to reach your target audience?

Are there people who will support this cause? Orchestrating a new model of ministry takes the combined energy and faith of many people. Do not take on the burden of such a process alone. Look over the available leadership. Is there a core group of people who are willing to pay the price to see the new model of ministry take place? If none can be found, begin to share your vision for a new model of ministry with key people, asking God to build a team of committed leaders.

Has the senior pastor been at your church long enough? As a rule of thumb, a pastoral tenure of more than four years is the minimum needed to bring about significant change. The only major exception to this rule occurs when a church is in a desperate situation. If that is the case, the rebirthed model may be the proper choice, and church leaders should move quickly to implement a new vision and direction for the church. Older, established churches give their full allegiance to church leaders only after the leadership has instilled confidence in the congregation through credible ministry. Do the people of the church trust the leaders? Has the senior pastor been at the church long enough to establish respect?

Are your pastor(s) and leaders willing to finish the job? Research in the field of church growth shows that it takes an average of seven years to implement significant changes in an urban or suburban church. Bringing about the same changes in a rural setting often takes ten to twelve years, if not longer. If the new model of ministry is successfully begun, will the senior pastor and other church leaders and staff remain at the church long enough to see it through to completion? It is unethical to lead the congregation to adopt a new form of ministry and then abandon it.

Is your church worth changing? Take a long look at the location of your church. Is it in the right location? If you were planting your church today, would you select its present site? If not, experience suggests it is wise not to put your people through the pain of change unless it will assist you in getting to the proper location. For example, an established church in a poor location would do best to start a satellite church in a more desirable location. This strategy allows a church to establish a point of ministry in the new place where it would rather be located.

Remodeling Your Church

Leading a church toward a new model of ministry requires more than a tweaking of the programs, by-laws, or worship service. Culture is what connects the mission of the church to the overall application of it in real life. The only way to translate vision and purpose into people's day-to-day behavior is to ground lofty concepts in the church's day-to-day environment.

Take Your Church Culture Seriously

All churches are immersed in culture—an identifiable atmosphere or climate in which the church operates. Culture is the sum total of the standard ways people are supposed to (and actually do) act within your church. At its basic level, culture is your church's personality. It is a below-the-surface reality that provides the glue, unity, and cohesion that makes your church unique. Cultural glue is comprised of four ingredients: behaviors, values, rules, and atmosphere.

- Behaviors—the routines of everyday church life, such as worshiping, decision making, and caregiving.
- Values—the core beliefs that function as a hidden force driving the church's decisions, often exposed in attitudes like tolerance, creativity, or inflexibility.
- Rules—the standardized ways of operating, such as by-laws, articles of incorporation, and a doctrinal statement.
- Atmosphere—the feel or environment that permeates the entire church.

Adopting a new model of ministry means capturing an entirely new church culture. Small or large changes in a church's programs will only touch the surface. The tough job is creating a new culture that supports the needed changes in ministry.[1] As you think about using new model of ministry, tailor your communication so that it speaks to all four aspects of your church's culture.

Stimulate a Passion for Change

The process of creating change is both simple and complex. It is at once easy to perceive but very difficult to bring about. Essentially, change can be explained by the equation $A + B + C - D$ = Change. Each element of this equation is defined as:

A—discontent
B—awareness of something better
C—understanding the first steps to take
D—cost of change

First, openness to a new model of ministry will arise when a church becomes discontented (A) with the present way of doing church. This is why it is crucial to contrast your church's purpose with its accomplishments. A church that does not fulfill its purpose should be discontented until it discovers a new model that is more effective. Second, a church must be aware of alternate models to use (B). Churches that are aware of only one or two approaches to church ministry need education and information on other models. Third, careful communication of the changes the church must make to implement a new model must be given (C). Once these three elements are understood, then the final cost of the change—financial, emotional, spiritual, and social (D)—is compared against the positive results the new model will bring. The bottom line? If the payoff is greater than the cost, then change will occur.

To stimulate a passion for change, keep the church's purpose and vision before the people. In every way possible, develop a passion to fulfill God's purpose in your church. Examine the progress your church has made in meeting its purpose and suggest alternate ways to be more effective.

Ask the Church to Experiment with the New Model

Once the people get comfortable and familiar with the new model, it stands a better chance of becoming permanent. Your goal is to capture a new culture that will be in place for a number of years. The satellite model is particularly good as an experiment, since it takes place away from the church property. If it does not succeed, it can be pulled back fairly easily without creating too much disruption.

Add, Don't Subtract

The principle of change is "Don't take away; add on." If a schism is taking place, you are moving too fast. Moving too quickly can hinder progress and undermine further attempts to remodel the church later on. The types of changes that are most effective are those that lift morale, build unity, and bring hope. In short, the best changes are those that are added to, not deleted from, what already exists. For many established churches, the seeker-sensitive, multiple-track, blended, and satellite models will be most appropriate, since they can be accomplished with a minimum of disruption to the standard practices of the church. Don't make people give up what is meaningful to them to start something that is meaningful to someone else. Assure them that you will continue to minister to them in the manner they are accustomed to.

Move Slower than You Want

In general, changes that take place quickly are short-lived, while a slower pace of change that establishes commitment is more permanent. Putting a new model of ministry into place actually takes place when all members have a part in causing it to happen. Acceptance of a new model of ministry grows through a predictable process. Originally defined by Dr. Win Arn, the process of accepting a new model of ministry travels through the following stages:

1. *Ignorance:* People are unaware of the present status of the church and of any need for a new model.

2. *Information:* People are informed of the current situation and the alternatives available.
3. *Infusion:* A new sense of faith and hope begins to be visible in the congregation.
4. *Individual acceptance:* People throughout the congregation begin to accept the need for a new model of ministry.
5. *Corporate acceptance:* The congregation as a whole accepts and backs the need for a new model of ministry.
6. *Awkward application:* The new model of ministry is attempted, resulting in normal mistakes and adaptations.
7. *Integration:* The new model is fully integrated into the life of the church, becoming the standard way of doing ministry.
8. *Innovation:* The church regularly develops new models of ministry in order to effectively fulfill its purpose.

Instituting any new ministry in a church requires that it pass through each and every one of these stages. As church leaders envision a new future for the church, they naturally go through these steps earlier than the members of the larger congregation. Then, when it comes time to introduce the new ministry to the people, there is a distance between where the leaders are in their thinking and where the congregation is in its thinking. In their desire to bring the congregation up to speed, leaders attempt to leapfrog the process by moving rapidly through stages one to four. Unless the congregation is desperate, this attempt to accelerate acceptance may backfire. If, and when, a schism begins to develop, it clearly indicates the process is moving too fast. It is always best to move slower than one wants to in order to allow the individual members of the congregation to progress through each stage.

Build Ownership among the People

Ownership of a new idea builds slowly over one to two years. About 2 percent of all church members will accept a new approach of ministry in the first three months of its introduction. Called innovators or dreamers, these people like change and are energized by new ways of doing ministry. Oscar Wilde defined such an individual as, "One who can only find his way by moonlight, and his punishment is that he sees the dawn before the rest of the world." While innovators see the future before others, it is a mistake to move with only their support (see figure 12).

Another 18 percent of the congregation will welcome the new model within six to nine months. These early adopters offer early encouragement and leadership to educate the remainder of the congregation.

It takes twelve to eighteen months to capture the commitment of the middle adopters. More cautious than the first 20 percent to accept the new model of ministry, they eventually agree to the new idea once they have had time to consider it at length.

The later adopters resist the concept of a new form of ministry for up to two years before finally acknowledging that it may indeed be workable. In the meantime they tolerate the 80 percent of the congregation who have excitedly moved forward, with or without them.

Much like a marathon race, there always are some stragglers who never quite seem to finish with the rest of the group. This final 2 percent of the congregation may never completely concur with the new approach to ministry but endure it since there is nothing else to do.

Start building ownership by focusing on individual people rather than groups. Call twelve to fifteen key members of your congrega-

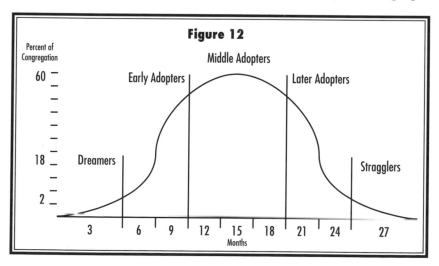

tion who are positive people. Schedule time to share your vision of a new model of ministry.

Follow up these meetings by scheduling lunch with fifteen to thirty people who may not support your ideas at first. Share your vision and ask them to think about it for a week. Then get back with them to get their feedback and answer any questions.

After meeting with numerous individuals, begin to meet with classes, boards, and committees to share your vision for a new model of ministry. Debrief their thoughts and ideas including additional information based on your lunch and phone conversations to further explain the new model.

Create Motion Rather than Explosion

Get the church moving toward the future, even if it is extremely slow. Don't move so fast that you create an explosion. If you hear negative reaction from the early adopters, you are definitely moving too fast. Build motion from the inside by using influence rather than from the outside by using authority. Forcing any concept, idea, or model on people from the position of authority will meet with heavy resistance. Leading through influence encounters less resistance, moving people along at their own pace.

Reward the Decision to Change

What gets praised gets done is the basic principle. Rewarding members for their willingness to risk starting a new model of ministry builds their pride and faith to accomplish more in the future. "Praise the behavior you want to

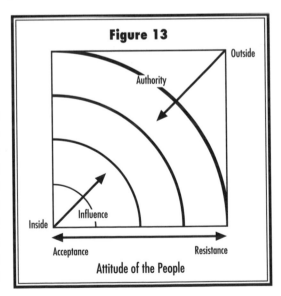

Figure 13

188

reinforce. The behavior that is reinforced is the behavior that is repeated. The behavior that is repeated becomes the prevailing attitude. The prevailing attitude becomes your church's culture."[2]

Keep the Vision before the People

On average people forget the purpose and vision behind the new model of ministry within four weeks. The work of communicating the "why" of your church's direction never ends. Communicate your vision repeatedly by using a memorable slogan. Find a story that expresses the heart of your purpose and then tell it over and over to your people. Project your vision for ministry through the use of videos and other media. Celebrate victories as they transpire. Communicate at every opportunity through everything you say and do.

Christ died, rose again, and lives today so that members of all generations can partake of salvation through his grace. The underlying intent of this book is to encourage you to explore fresh new models of ministry that are proving effective in evangelizing Boomers and Busters and assimilating them into the church. Rigidly repeating the models of yesterday can severely limit our churchs' ability to fulfill the Great Commission. Too much emphasis on tomorrow can put us in a paralyzing pattern of never ministering today. We must learn reverently from the past, dream great dreams for the future, and work today to reach our communities for Christ. Selecting one of the models outlined in this book can restore new life and vitality to your ministry. Now it is time to dream a new dream and . . . obey!

Notes

1: Over the Hill to Grandma's House

1. For a complete study of each generation, see the author's book *Three Generations: Riding the Waves of Change in Your Church* (Grand Rapids: Revell, 1995).

2. George Barna, *User Friendly Churches* (Ventura Calif.: Regal, 1991).

3. Dr. Robert E. Logan has produced numerous materials for church planting. For information on all his products write, call, or fax CHURCH-SMART Resources, 390 E. St. Charles Rd., Carol Stream, IL 60188, 800-253-4276, 630-871-8708 (FAX), E-mail: 103612.2011@compuserve.com.

2: Take My BMW, Please

1. The rock group The Who exclaimed in their 60s anthem, "My Generation," "I hope I die before I get old."

2. Joe Urschel, "As Boomers Hit 50, Can AARP Be Far Behind?" *Sun*, 4 June 1995, E3.

3. Shankar Vedantam, "Boomers Pass a Milestone in '96," *Sun*, 30 December 1995, A2.

4. "Survey: Boomers Moving to the Right," *Sun*, 18 February 1996, D1.

5. Dr. Win Arn, "A New Paradigm for Ministry: Middle Adults," *L.I.F.E. LINE*, 3, nd.

6. "Is Middle Age Creeping Up on You?" *USA Today Magazine* (July 1990): 7.

7. Jim Conway, *Men in Mid-Life Crisis* (Elgin, Ill.: David C. Cook, 1981), 49.

8. Alexandra Alger, "Nipping and Tucking," *Forbes* (4 December 1995): 290–92.

9. Marc Spiegler, "Knees Have No Warranties," *American Demographics* (July 1995): 21.

10. "News/Trends," *Fortune* (21 September 1992): 13.

11. Vedantam, "Boomers Pass a Milestone in '96," A1.

12. "How Baby Boomers Are Coping with Life Changes," *Sun*, 28 January 1990, E2.

13. Maria Blackburn, "Less Is Becoming More a Way of Life," *Sun*, 18 December 1995, D6.

14. Ibid.

15. "Miracles of Marketing," *Success* (April 1993): 20.

16. Ibid., 25.

17. Vedantam, "Boomers Pass a Milestone in '96," A1.

18. "Baby Boomers Watch Spending, Survey Says," *Sun*, 16 July 1995, D1.

19. John Manners, "Searching for Paradise Lost," *Money* (March 1993): 138–39.

20. Paul Glastris, "The New Way to Get Rich," *U.S. News and World Report* (7 May 1990): 27–36.

21. Cheryl Russell, "Boomer Nest Eggs," *American Demographics* (July 1995): 8.

22. George H. Gallup Jr. and Robert Bezilla, "A Boom in Religion," *Sun*, 27 February 1994, D4.

23. Stephen R. Covey, *The 7 Habits of Highly Effective People* (New York: Simon & Schuster, 1989).

24. Julia Lawlor, "Clan of the '7 Habits,'" *USA Weekend* (12–24 January 1996): 4.

25. Trudi Miller Rosenblum, "Spiritual Exercise Videos Catch On," *Sun*, 15 July 1995, D1.

26. Ibid.

27. Randall Rothenberg, "Yesterday Looms Large in Baby Boomers' Minds," *New York Times*, nd, E1.

28. George Barna, "The Case of the Missing Boomers," *Ministry Currents* (January–March 1992): 2.

29. Phillip Longman, "Don't Blame the Boomers," *My Generation* (newsletter of the American Association of Boomers, 433 E. Los Colinas Blvd., Suite 240, Irving, TX 75039), fall 1993, 9.

30. Anita Manning, "Boomer Power Is Top '96 Trend," *Sun*, 17 December 1995, E3.

31. Dr. Elmer Towns, in a seminar, "How to Reach the Baby Boomers," lists seven reasons Boomers will be open to church as they grow older.

1. They will return to church as other generations have to teach values to their children; provide services for family; and to relate to other parents of like-goals and like-problems.
2. They will return to church as other generations have due to a desire for stability, nostalgia, and value.
3. They will return to church as other generations have as they become assimilated into the institutions of business, family, school, and government, leading naturally to identify with the church, another institution.
4. They will return to church as other generations have as a symbol of belonging, acceptance, and identity.
5. They will return to church as other generations have because they are "burned out" on the popular culture and will seek to identify with enduring and lasting values.
6. They will return to church as other generations have because they are seeking ultimate reality in "spirit" realms, whether Eastern religions, New Age Movement, traditional churches, or new emerging conservative churches.
7. They will return to church as other generations have because they are insecure about the future and are frightened and confused.

32. David Briggs, "Boomers Shun Church When Children Leave," *Press Enterprise*, 9 September 1994.

33. Cathy Lynn Grossman, "December Offers Chance to Reflect on Religion in Your Life," *Sun*, 20 December 1992, E3.

34. Barna, "The Case of the Missing Boomers," 2.

35. Wendy Dennis, "The Baby Boom Blues," *Toronto Life* 24, no. 3 (February 1990): 50–65.

3: Generation X-Cellent

1. Nicholas Zill and John Robinson, "The Generation X Difference," *American Demographics* (April 1995): 24–26.

2. Cheryl Russell and Susan Mitchell, "Talking about Whose Generation?" *American Demographics* (April 1995): 33.

3. The reader is once again referred to the author's book *Three Generations: Riding the Waves of Change in Your Church* (Grand Rapids: Revell, 1995) for a complete study of the Buster generation.

4. Barbara Bradley, "Marketing That New-Time Religion," *Los Angeles Times Magazine* (10 December 1995): 54.

5. Curt Schleier, "Marriage, Music Keep Chynna Phillips Busy," *Sun*, 2 January 1996, D4.

6. Helaine Olen, "Boomer Backlash: Women Say They'll Put Family First," *Los Angeles Times Orange County Edition*, 12 June 1991, E6.

7. Liesel Walsh, "Why the Baby Bust Won't Spend," *American Demographics* (December 1992): 14.

8. "Baby Busters Following Most Traditional Patterns," *Emerging Trends* (published by the Princeton Research Center, P.O. Box 389, Princeton, NJ 08542) 16, no. 2 (February 1994): 3.

9. Ibid.

10. Charles Arn, "Why Baby Busters Don't Go to Church," *The Win Arn Growth Report*, nd.

11. Gary L. McIntosh, "Baby Busters: Update 1991," *The Church Growth Network* 3, no. 11 (November 1991): 1.

12. John Naisbitt, *Megatrends* (New York: Warner Communications Co., 1984), 269.

4: The Choice of a New Generation

1. Zill and Robinson, "The Generation X Difference," 27.

2. Fred Newell, cited in *Arthur Andersen Retailing Issues Letter* (nd), Center for Retailing Studies, Texas A&M University, College Station, TX 77843.

3. Gene Getz, *Sharpening the Focus of the Church* (Wheaton, Ill.: Victor, 1984), 273.

4. "Research Expert Gives Strategies on Reaching the Unchurched," *Southern California Times* (October 1991): 14.

5. Mark Galli, "Learning to Be Some Things to Some People," *Leadership* (fall 1991): 37.

6. Ibid.

7. Ibid.

8. Martin E. Marty, "Challenge to Congregations: Become Interesting," *The Lutheran* (6 January 1988): 9.

9. Getz, *Sharpening the Focus of the Church*, 283.

10. John R. W. Stott, *Between Two Worlds* (Grand Rapids: Eerdmans, 1982), 55.

11. Kent Hunter, "Reaching Baby Boomers and Baby Busters with the Gospel," *Church*

Growth Foundation Newsletter (spring 1991): 3, P.O. Box 468, Charleston, TN 37310.

12. Adapted from Gary L. McIntosh, "Reaching Baby Boomers: Part 2," *The McIntosh Church Growth Network* 1, no. 3 (March 1989): 1–2.

13. *Journal for Adult Education* 3, no. 2 (1991): 30.

5: The Seeker-Centered Model

1. Tom Valeo, "The Drama of Willow Creek," *Chicago Daily Herald*, 19 May 1988, sec. 9, p. 3.

2. For a complete discussion of selecting a new church name, see Gary L. McIntosh, *The Exodus Principle* (Nashville: Broadman & Holman, 1995), 120–23.

3. Valeo, "The Drama of Willow Creek," 3.

6: A Look at a Seeker-Centered Church

1. Burt Nanus, *Visionary Leadership* (San Francisco: Jossey-Bass, 1992), 3.

7: The Seeker-Sensitive Model

1. Adapted from *California Approaches to Reaching Unchurched "Baby Boomers,"* distributed by the California Southern Baptist Convention, 678 East Shaw Ave., Fresno, CA 93710.

2. Thom S. Rainer, *Giant Awakenings* (Nashville: Broadman & Holman, 1995), 135.

3. I first wrote about guesterizing a church in *The Exodus Principle*, 151–59.

4. Rainer, *Giant Awakenings*, 123.

5. Ibid., 48.

6. Ibid., 81.

7. Bradley, "Marketing That New-Time Religion," 33.

8. Rainer, *Giant Awakenings*, 55.

9. Ibid., 48.

10. Bradley, "Marketing That New-Time Religion," 33.

9: The Blended Model

1. Rainer, *Giant Awakenings*, 171.

2. Ibid.

3. McIntosh, *Three Generations*, 182.

4. Rainer, *Giant Awakenings*, 171–72.

10: A Look at a Blended Church

1. William M. Easum, *Sacred Cows Make Gourmet Burgers* (Nashville: Abingdon Press, 1995). Also, for a comparison of the changes in church ministry see McIntosh, *The Issachar Factor.*

12: A Look at a Multiple-Track Church

1. Adapted from Josh Hunt, *Let It Grow!* (Grand Rapids: Baker, 1993), 182.

13: The Satellite Model

1. Rainer, *Giant Awakenings*, 151.

2. Elmer L. Towns, ed., *A Practical Encyclopedia of Evangelism and Church Growth* (Ventura, Calif.: Regal, 1995), 348.

3. C. Peter Wagner, *Church Planting for a Greater Harvest* (Ventura, Calif.: Regal, 1990), 66.

4. Elmer L. Towns, *10 of Today's Most Innovative Churches* (Ventura, Calif.: Regal, 1990).

17: Remodeling Your Church

1. For added information on creating a new church culture, see McIntosh, *The Exodus Principle.*

2. Ibid., 195.